Three Summer Herbs

Over 100 Plant-based Recipes

for Herb Lovers

by Gail Herndon Huskins

Cover design by Courtney Brillhart
courtneybrillhart.com

ISBN: 978-1-7327081-4-3
Library of Congress Control Number 2018910500

This book is dedicated to my husband,

who not only had the big idea for this book,

but ate his way through it

Table of Contents

Introduction

I love herbs. I love using them in the kitchen, of course, but also tucked in a pillowcase, thrown into warm bath water, added to a floral bouquet, or tied with an organza ribbon to an otherwise plainly wrapped present. They are beautiful to look at and transcendent to breathe in. Herbs are the B-side to flowers--nature's true aromatherapy.

Everybody has a favorite herb. It's rare to take inventory in a room full of people and hear an herb mentioned twice. After all, there are so many to love! And people are passionate about their beloved herb. The mere mention can make them smile. Anyone breathing in deeply? Sublime. Herbal scents show up everywhere--from bath soaps and air fresheners to dish detergents and anti-static dryer sheets to holiday potpourri. And no wonder. Fragrance has the ability to transport us to another place. Another *lovely* place. That's something to hold on to.

My wise sister-in-law Susan described it best: "Rosemary makes my heart sing." I get that, and if you picked up this book, you likely do too. Whatever makes your heart sing, do more of that.

Why I Wrote This Book

This book came about because I garden and grow a lot of herbs. Sometimes I have an over-abundance. It's a situation many home gardeners experience, usually accompanied by the borderline panic that sets with the realization you need to use something up, and fast. Pesto is great, but I longed for a broader collection of recipes for my herbs—something new, exciting and different. I started collecting recipes and began experimenting. I taught cooking classes, focused on a single herb, that would conclude with a 4 or 5-course meal of sweet and savory dishes (and an occasional cocktail). I met a wonderful community of people who share a love and enthusiasm for herbs. Teaching with a single focus helped me organize my thoughts about an herb, and this method resonated with others. Because of the popularity of those classes, my husband suggested I turn the coursework into a book. This is the first in a series of four cookbooks featuring seasonal herbs.

Three Summer Herbs is a diverse collection of the very best recipes that showcase the enchanting flavors of the season: Lavender, Basil and Cilantro.

Kitchen Assists

Having the right tool for the job is important, but it's not everything. But before we get to tools, here are some practices that can help set you and your recipes up for success.

Practice *mise en place*
Translation: Everything in its place. (Thank the French.) It's all about preparing and organizing your work space, before you start to cook. It's not simply having all your ingredients and measuring cups out. It's having everything measure and chopped or toasted, and having all the bowls and utensils out before you start to cook. This gives you more flow in the kitchen and saves time. No more grabbing a drawer handle with dough on your hands because you forgot to set out a spatula.

Read the recipe method through before making it
This is Boy Scout Motto stuff: *Always Be Prepared*. It's not enough to skim the ingredient list, and mentally check that you have all the necessary ingredients. In addition, read the recipe method so there are no surprises or delays in preparing your dish. Sadly, not all ingredient lists mention that the raisins need to be soaked, the grains cooled or the nuts toasted. Know what you're getting yourself into.

Set aside time (and times) to cook
I threw a lot of food away in my 20s. I had the best of intentions, but poor execution. Looking back, I clearly see my problem. I didn't plan. Planning was a responsible adult behavior, and one I had yet to master. I wanted to be free and flexible, and buy whatever inspired me; whatever produce was good, fresh and ripe. I mistook flexibility for poor planning. I didn't shop

with a list, didn't plan what I would make, and didn't plan when I would make it. That's pretty much a blueprint to waste money and throw away food.

Planning is key. If you aren't in the habit, start where you are. Set a small goal to cook one night a week, and plan to get at least two meals out of it. Or set a goal to block out little chunks of time. Can you wash and prep some veggies? Chop the onion, carrots and celery so they'll be ready later when you need them? Make the dressing today for tomorrow's meal? Toast nuts or throw rice in the rice cooker? Look at a recipe by breaking it down by components. Identify that one thing that you can do in a small amount of time that will lighten the load later, and then do it. If you can do two, or have a helper in the kitchen, all the better.

Optional Cooking Enhancers
Music. Wine. *#'NuffSaid*

If you don't grow veggies, buy fresh, organic ingredients whenever possible.
They may be a tad more expensive, but they have more nutrients, and you can actually taste the difference. Don't believe me? Try it. *#OrganicTastesBetter*

Sources for fresh, organic veggies are your local CSA (Community Supported Agriculture) and farmer's markets. You'll find a variety of seasonal fruit and veggies grown locally and they're typically cheaper than at the supermarket.

Want to do your own picking? PickYourOwn.org lets you search for farms in your area (U.S. and abroad) that let you do the harvesting. That can save some cash and make for a fun outing.

FallingFruit.org is an open-source database of all kinds of food grown on public lands. I learned about some blackberries growing near a jogging trail close to me. This is a great resource for the "contemporary forager." *#AddThatToYourResume*

A Note About Ingredients

Aquafaba, jackfruit, ackee, nutritional yeast, nigella seeds, soy curls, kelp granules, vanilla paste, agar-agar...I'm hoping not *all* of these are new to you, but if they are, don't despair. (And if they are, this will be fun.) The majority of the recipes do not call for an odd component; however, there will be an occasional new ingredient. More and more, traditional supermarket chains across the country carry them. If not, you can find them at your neighborhood health food store, Whole Foods, or international markets. If you don't have convenient access to any of those, there is Amazon. *#Groceries:Delivered*

Eating Plant-Based

If you're new to the world of plant-based foods, it's a really great time because there are so many products to choose from, in just about all food categories. There are a lot of players already in the plant-based foods market, and the sector is growing. Which means your options are only going to get better, and better tasting. Here are some readily available store-bought foods that you can find at major supermarkets, major superstores, natural food stores, international markets, or directly from the manufacturer. Visit their websites for ingredient and nutritional information and recipes. Many of the smaller brands have forms, scripts and/or links to supermarket chains so you can readily request that their products be carried near you.

Keep a little inventory in your freezer or cupboards to help make meal planning easier. This isn't a complete list but gives you an idea of what's available already. As you discover new brands, be sure to read the ingredient list—some manufacturers make both vegetarian and vegan products.

<u>Bacon and Pork</u>
Gardein Porkless Bites
Lightlife Smart Bacon and Fakin' Bacon®
McCormick Bac'n Pieces Bacon Flavored Bits
Phoney Baloney's Coconut Bacon (several flavors in pouches)
Sweet Earth Natural Foods® Benovelent Bacon and Harmless Ham
Tofurkey® Tempeh Bacon and Ham Style Roast
Upton Naturals® Seitan Bacon

Beef and Burgers (several flavors within most brands)
The Alternative Meat Co.® Beef Free Chunks
Amy's Kitchen
Beyond Meat® The Beyond Burger (ready-to-cook)
Beyond Meat® Beast Burger (frozen patty)
Boca's Vegan Burger
Dr. Praeger's® veggie burger (gluten-free)
Engine 2® Plant Strong® Plant Burgers
Field Roast® Fieldburger
Gardein Chipolte Black Bean Burger, Beefless Burger, Sliders
Gardein Beefless Tips
Gardenburger®
Hilary's Eat Well (all gluten and soy-free)
Impossible Foods Impossible Burger (Kosher certification)
Lightlife Smart Burgers®
Morningstar Farms Vegan Burger®
Atlantic Natural Foods's Neat meat replacement mix (gluten-free)
Qrunch Organics Foods Quinoa Burger (gluten-free)
Quorn Vegan Burgers (not all are vegan)
Sweet Earth Natural Foods® Veggie Burger
Sunshine Burgers® (all gluten-free)
Trader Joe's® Beefless Ground Beef
Upton's Naturals Burger Patties

Burritos (several flavors within each brand)
Alpha Foods burrito
Daiya Burritos
Engine 2® Plant Strong® organic burritos
Sweet Earth Natural Foods® (not all are vegan)

Butter
Chao Creamery (part of Field Roast®) Buttery Spread (tub)
Earth Balance® Buttery Spread (sticks and tubs)
I Can't Believe It's Not Butter® vegan spread (tub)
Melt® Organic Buttery Spread (sticks and tubs)
Miyoko's European Style Cultured Vegan Butter (stick)

Cheese (several flavors within most brands)
Miyoko's cheese wheels
Chao Creamery Slices (part of Field Roast®)
Daiya cheese (shreds, blocks, sticks and frozen pizza)
Heidi Ho! Organics (tubs)
Kite Hill Artisan Almond Milk Foods
So Delicious® Shreds (pouch)
Tofutti® Better Than Ricotta Cheese®

Cream Cheese and Sour Cream
Kite Hill Artisan Almond Milk Foods Cream Cheese Style Spread
Tofutti® Better Than Cream Cheese®
Tofutti® Better Than Sour Cream®

Chicken (several flavors within most brands) (In freezer section if not noted)
The Alternative Meat Co.® Chicken Free Strips
Beyond Meat® Chicken-Free Strips
Boca Spicy Chick'n Patties and Nuggets
Gardein (crispy chick'n, fingers, strips, tenders)
Loma Linda® FriChik Original and Tender Bits (both canned)

Quorn Chik'n Tenders, Patties and Cutlets (not all Quorn products are vegan)

Tofurkey® Slow Roasted Chick'n

Crab/Fish/Scallops (In freezer section if not noted)
Gardein Crabless Cakes and Fishless Filets
Loma Tuno or Fishless Tuna (canned)
Loma Linda® Vegetable Skallops (canned)
Quorn Fishless Sticks
Sophie's Kitchen Vegan Toona (canned); crab cakes, fish, scallops and shrimp)

Egg replacement, (baking) when applesauce, flaxmeal, tofu or a banana won't do
Atlantic Natural Foods The Neat Egg (pouch)
Bob's Red Mill® Egg Replacer (gluten-free) (pouch)
Ener-G® Egg Replacer (box)

Egg replacement, (scrambles, frittata and quiche)
Follow Your Heart® Vegan Egg (mini-egg carton container)
Just Inc. (formerly Hampton Creek) Just Egg (squeeze container)
Vegg Vegan Egg Yolk (pouch)

Honey (several flavors within most brands)
Bee Free Honee® (gluten-free)
Peaceful Planet Vegan Hunny
Plant-Based Artisan Vegan Honea

Hotdogs (several flavors within most brands)
Field Roast® Frankfurters
Lightlife Tofu Pups®, Smart Dogs® and Jumbo Smart Dogs®
Loma Linda® Big Franks and Linketts (canned)
Yves® Veggie Cuisine Veggie Dogs

Ice Cream (several flavors within most brands)
Almond Dream
Ben & Jerry's (Buyer Beware: most are not vegan)
Blue Mountain Organics Cashew Creamery
Luna & Larry's Coconut Bliss®
Nada Moo! (coconut-based)
Snow Monkey Superfood Ice Treat
So Delicious® (coconut, almond and soy)
Tofutti® Frozen Dessert
Trader Joe's® Soy Creamy

Mayonnaise (several flavors within most brands)
Chao Creamery (part of Field Roast®) Original Mayo
Follow Your Heart® Veganaise (plus tartar sauce and horseradish)
Just Inc. Mayo

Meatless Ground, Steaks, Cutlets, Chunks, Granules and Texturized Vegetable Protein
Bob's Red Mill® TVP® (bag)
Elianni Veggie Cutlets (boxed dehydrated cutlets made from soybeans and pinto beans)
Fearn Soya Granules (oatmeal-type canister)
Gardein Beefless Ground (freezer section)

Lightlife Smart Ground Crumbles® (freezer section)
Lightlife Gimme Lean Smart Menu Veggie Meatballs®
Lightlife Veggie Beef® (freezer section)
Loma Linda (part of Atlantic Natural Foods; Prime Stakes (canned)
Now® Foods Textured Soy Protein Granules (pouch)
Nutrela® High Protein Soy (boxed dehydrated chunks and granules)

Meatballs, Meatloaf and Roasts
Field Roast® has several varieties of loaves and a Classic Meatloaf
Gardein Meatless Meatballs and Meatless Meatloaf
Lightlife® Smart Menu Meatballs

Milk/Creamer/Half and Half (many flavors within most brands)
Banana Wave® Banana Milk
Blue Diamond Almond Breeze® Almond Milk
Earth Balance® Soy Milk and Soy Nog
EcoMil® Quinoa Milk
Edensoy®
Good Karma Flax Milk
Living Harvest Tempt Hemp Milk
Milkadamia Macadamia Milk
Oatly! Oat Milk
Pacific Foods Non Dairy Beverage (nuts and seed milks)
Ripple (pea milk)
Rice Dream® Rice Drink
Silk®
So Delicious®
Soy Dream soymilk (and rice, nut and blends)
Sunrich Natural SōL Sunflower Beverage

Sunflower Dream Sunflower Drink
Trader Joe's®
WestSoy®
Whole Foods Market 365

Pizza
Amy's Kitchen (cheese, no cheese and gluten-free options)
Daiya (several flavors and toppings)
Tofurkey® Pizza (gluten-free)
Sweet Earth Natural Foods® Veggie Lover's Pizza (others are vegetarian)
Whole Foods 365 Vegan Pizza

Ravioli
Engine 2® Plant Strong®

Sausage and Chorizo (many flavors within most brands)
Beyond Meat® Beyond Sausage®
Field Roast® Breakfast Sausage
Gardein Breakfast Saus'age Patties
Hilary's Eat Well Breakfast Sausage (soy and gluten-free)
Tofurkey® sausage
Yves® Veggie Cuisine sausages

Seitan (many flavors within most brands)
Pacific Foods Seitan
Sweet Earth Natural Foods® (strips, slices, ground, satay)
Upton's Natural®
West Soy® (strips, cubes, chicken style, ground)

Shortening
Earth Balance® shortening (sticks)
Nutiva® Shortening (tub)
Spectrum® Organic Vegetable Shortening (tub)

Turkey
Gardein Turk'y Cutlet
Tofurkey® Roast

Worcestershire sauce
Annie's Naturals® Organic Worcestershire Sauce
Robbie's Worcestershire Sauce

Yogurt (many flavors within each brand)
Good Karma yogurt (flax milk)
Kite Hill® European and Greek-style (almond milk)
Ripple Greek Yogurt Alternative (pea milk)
Soy Dream yogurt (soy milk)
So Delicious® yogurt (coconut milk)

So there you go. Plenty of good tasting, dairy-free, egg-free and some soy and gluten-free foods to go nuts over. If you find something you like, ask your grocery store to carry it.

Kitchen Gear

Before replacing any tool or making a first-time purchase, it's worth a stop in a large kitchenware store. Comparing items on Amazon only goes so far, though I do think that's an important part of the process. There's great benefit to seeing items up close and personal, and holding them in your own hands. The sales folks are another good resource. Chat 'em up about which products get returned most often, or which ones remain popular, year after year.

Apple corer

There's no other tool that can quickly cut through the core of a whole apple, and keep it in one piece. Look for a stainless steel with a serrated end, and one that opens along the side, or has an open section on the side. This is an improvement over the solid column type, which make it really hard to get the core out. to get rid of the core quicker. Use it to core pears too.

Bamboo steamer

You might be surprised that I consider a bamboo steamer a *must-have* kitchen tool, but think about it. These stackable trays mean you've got more surface area for steaming. If you're making dumplings or won tons, it's a whole lot nicer to steam them all at once than to batch cook (or at least do fewer batches). But it's also great for reheating food, steaming veggies, and bringing hard or stale bread back to life.

Battery-operated flour sifter

What a great invention this is, I LOVE it. The metal ones are awkward to use, particularly the crank variety, and make me feel like I need a third hand. Over time, they get grody and rust and never really clean thoroughly. My new sifter can hold 5 cups of flour, with a bottom screen that easily twists off for quick clean up. I'm not happy that it's plastic, but it's still an improvement. I prefer it to the squeeze-handle types.

Box grater

A stainless steel box grater is easy to grab for small jobs, like grating ½ an apple for muesli or shredding leftover vegetable pieces for salads or a tofu scramble. There's no need to dirty a food processor for such small amounts.

Cast iron skillet

From cornbread to quiche, every kitchen should have a cast iron skillet. Aside from the nice oven-to-table presentation, cooking in cast iron can boost your dietary iron intake. *#FreeGiftWithPurchase*

Cheesecloth

A package of 100% unbleached cotton cheesecloth will last for years. It's super inexpensive and vital for transforming plain non-dairy yogurt into thick, Greek-style, or infusing herbs and spices in wine, tea or soups. No more biting into a whole peppercorn or cardamom pod. Bundling everything into a piece of cheesecloth avoids that.

Chef's knife

If you only have one "good" knife in the kitchen, make it a chef's knife. It's the most versatile knife you'll own. They are eight or ten inches in length, with a slight curve to the blade. Preference varies, not just in length but weight. It needs to feel right in your hand --not too heavy or too light. You could spend a lot of money, but certainly don't have to. Google various food blogs to learn their latest recommendations and features, costs, and where to find them. Hold several in your hand before making a decision.

Colander

I got a set of three collapsible colanders at CostCo and use them for rinsing fruit, veggies, salad greens and draining pasta. I love that they nestle inside one another so they don't take up much storage space.

Crock pot

This is one of my best friends in the winter. Next to a rice cooker, it's any working woman's secret kitchen helper. I haven't found a soup yet that can't be made in a crock pot. Just throw everything in and go. Deliciousness wafts through the air and greets you when you return home. *#CrockpotsAreSelfCare*

Dumpling press

Watching Chinese chefs deftly pinch and fold little bite size portions of dough and create dim sum is one of the wonders of the food world. My folding skills are so not there, but I can fake it with a dumpling press. They make the whole process go faster, and your dumplings will look next to perfect. If you have a few presses, invite some friends over, divide the work and share the dumplings. *#TheyHaveDumplingMakingPartiesDon'tThey?*

Fine-mesh strainer

These are essential for rinsing canned beans, rice and grains, and straining off herbs used in an infusion. Keep a couple of sizes at the ready. Small strainers are perfect for rinsing delicate herbs and sprouts.

Flexible cutting mats

Wooden cutting boards are beautiful, but you'll have better functionality with flexible mats. I set out two to four of them every time I cook. It's one easy movement to pick up and transfer a mat of diced veggies or minced herbs into a pot on the stove. Plus, they don't take up as much storage space.

Food processor
Food processors are the best choice for processing ingredients that don't require the smoothness a high-speed blender provides, but they have plenty of other uses. The interchangeable grating disc allows you to quickly and more uniformly grate vegetables than a box grater would.

Garlic press
I've gone through several in my years in the kitchen, but my favorite is a Joseph Joseph garlic rocker press, (yes, the brand is two of the same name). It's a single curved piece of stainless steel that you place on top of a clove of garlic and press. I find it easier to push than to squeeze, and this one is also a lot easier to clean.

Glass bowls
A couple of different sizes of small glass bowls are essential for *mise en place*. I have half a dozen of two sizes, and they double as serving bowls for garnishments and other smaller items.

High-speed blender
I am loyal to my Vitamix, but there are several other brands that my friends swear by. Whatever your choice, this is another staple kitchen item because there are so many things you can use it for. They can be pricey, but they're a worthwhile investment. They're indispensable for getting a smooth end product, such as sauces, creams and purées.

Kitchen scale

Invariably, some recipes call for the weight of an item that isn't packaged and sold in the supermarket. Take the guesswork out of it and get a scale. Weight is the most accurate method of measuring flour when baking, and, if you use an app like *My Fitness Pal* to count calories, calculating your food intake just got easier. Google food blogs to learn their recommendations.

Kitchen shears

Kitchen scissors make cutting herbs super easy, especially the ones with 5-blades. Occasionally, my quality control isn't 100% and I'll see a long herbal stalk floating in a stock pot. I can stick the scissors in the pot, and a couple of snips will take care of it.

Lemon juicer

I prefer the manual, table-top variety that catch the juices in a container. I'm frequently juicing for more than one recipe, or to have a little extra for a cup of warm water in the mornings. Look for one with interchangeable reamers, to accommodate oranges and limes.

Mandoline

A mandoline can cut wafer-thin, delicate slices that are unlike anything cut with a knife. Super thin slices are desired when baking veggie chips, prepping raw foods or dehydrating vegetables. Truth be told, I have cut a finger. OK two. I've cut two fingers with my mandoline. Nothing that required a trip to the hospital, but let me just say using a mandoline requires the utmost caution and focus. For the best insurance, get yourself some cut-resistant kitchen gloves. Basily makes an inexpensive pair.

Microplane

A problem using a hand grater is that zest, for example, flies all over the place. Because of its narrow shape, the microplane solves that problem by focusing the zest in one location. This is the best tool to grate ginger or get zest from citrus.

Mortar and pestle

This tool has the ability to coax out more of an herb's essential oil than a food processor can. Granted, mashing by hand is a slower process, but it won't heat up the herb, and heat is a delicate herb's enemy, transforming their bright colors into a very unappetizing brown–black. Keep both the herb's colors and flavors more alive by using a mortar and pestle. It's really great for combining an herb with another ingredient, such as lavender and sugar or chives and sea salt. If you have a larger size mortar and pestle, try your hand at hand-mashed pesto or guacamole. Let me know if you can see and taste the difference.

Rice cooker

This is a great time-saving appliance, and now that I cook an occasional "pancake" in it, its usefulness has expanded. Get a big one or little one, and use it to cook all your grains: any kind of rice, freekeh, quinoa, millet, oat groats, or buckwheat. Most come with a convenient steamer basket that fits over the rice. I use mine at least once a week.

Silicone freezer trays

You know when a recipe calls for 2 tablespoons of tomato paste? What happens to the rest of the little can? Until I discovered these little trays, I'd prefer not to tell you. Now I scoop the leftovers in 1 or 2 tablespoon amounts into these trays and freeze for future use. Ditto for canned coconut milk and the occasional remnants of a bottle of wine...

Flexible baby food freezer trays will also do the job.

Silpat baking mats and parchment paper

Truly, there is a place for both. Parchment get things more browned on the bottom, (think roasted vegetables), whereas silicone, because of its thickness, offers more protection, for some of the more delicate baked goods. Both provide an easy clean up. *#CanIGetAnAmen?*

Spice grinder

You can pick up a new coffee bean grinder or re-purpose an old one, and dedicate it to herbs and spices. Be sure to clean well after each use, to keep flavors from intermingling.

Spider strainer

I initially bought a spider strainer (aka mesh or spider skimmer) to use when making tempura and other batter-fried foods. It has a wide, wire base that easily scoops through oil and facilitates fast draining. Then I found I used it a lot to remove herbs when I infuse them in soups, alcohol or syrups. Get one that's 10" long, so you won't miss anything lingering along the bottom of a deep stockpot.

Squeeze bottles

You can find the classic red and yellow squeeze bottles for ketchup and mustard at your local grocery store, or smaller sizes with no identifying color. They're perfect when you want a more artistic or controlled portion of say, coconut cream on soup, infused mayo on an open-faced sandwich, or chocolate sauce on a slice of pie. Swirling two colors of sauce is even better.

Stick or immersion blender

Batching soup in a high-speed blender can be a pain. Depending on the smoothness of your end product, a stick blender may save you the hassle. Choose a brand that includes other attachments, like whisks or a small beaker container for making things like salad dressings. A stick blender is one of the best tools of the modern kitchen.

Unbleached wax paper

Look for non-toxic, biodegradable, unbleached wax paper, made with soybean wax instead of paraffin. Paraffin wax is petroleum-based and non-renewable. It's found in most other (and certainly our mother's generation) wax paper. I found a brand called *If You Care,* that makes their packaging from recycled cardboard, and it's printed with vegetable-based inks. *#ProvingThatTheyCare*

Vegetable peeler

I've used swivel peelers, Y-peelers and the weird small finger peeler, and I always come back to the swivel. (You peel away from your body with the swivel; towards your body with the Y-peeler. The latter are allegedly easier for lefties.) It's a necessary tool for peeling potatoes, carrots or making zucchini or cucumber ribbons.

Whisk

There are several kinds of whisks, but I think you can limit the "must-haves" to at most three. It's worth noting that some are silicone-coated, and depending on your pans, may be preferred to help extend their life.

For whipping and incorporating air, choose a balloon whisk. Its exaggerated, round shape (think: hot air balloon) helps whip more air into the mix, creating a light, whipped finished product such as coconut whipped cream. Balloon whisks can be used with dry ingredients as well, to aerate flour instead of using a flour sifter.

For blending ingredients, select a French whisk. They look like a more elegant, tapered version of the balloon whisk. These are a good choice when making batters and heavier sauces.

An optional third whisk is the flat or roux whisk. It looks like a French whisk that's been stepped on. The shape allows you to more easily scrape the bottom of a pan, and get at the edges better. As the name indicates, these are the best pick when making a roux for sauces, soups or gravy.

Those are my three, but I have to mention one more: the coil whisk. It's just a thicker single wire wrapped into a round coil shape. It's used more like a pump, in an up–and–down motion. You know, like a pogo stick, but for your hand. It's hard to take anyone seriously when they are making that motion, particularly in the kitchen with their hand inside a pot. *#JustDon't*

How to Use This Book

It's not organized like other cookbooks

The recipes aren't organized in the traditional sense--with standard categories like Appetizers, Sides, Entrees, etc. In fact, there is no recipe listing. This is intentional. That's because I can't predict what kind of *Food Mood* I'm going to be in. If you're someone who reads a lot and has "book moods", that's similar. I like to try new things and can't tell you what I'll feel like making until I see it. *#Don'tBoxMeIn*

This deliberate "unconventional" organization just might prove helpful

Taking recipes out of their "normal" categories makes you see them differently. I perceive a lot of fluidity between food categories anyway. Salads can be main dishes, veggies can be turned into an entrée, and a snack or side dish can be enough for a complete meal. If I go out to eat, I'm typically creating a dinner from 2-3 starters or side dishes. That's the spirit to think about with these recipes.

Serving size is relative

If you're like me, you've been burned by trusting a recipe's stated serving size. It's a pet peeve of mine. I'd rather you tell me how many cups a recipe makes so I can more realistically predict how many people that's going to serve. Sometimes I give you both the quantity in cups as well as a serving size, so you can better gage how a recipe will work for you.

Taste and adjust seasoning

This is super important. Every recipe should have this somewhere in the directions, and if you've not paid attention before, get in the habit of tasting throughout the cooking process. That's when you have the chance to correct and balance the flavors. This is key. I've made every recipe several times, which means I've got them to my taste…which may not be to your taste. Taste for the balance of salt, sweet, acid, the herb, etc. Adjust until you are happy with the flavor. *#AlwaysTasteAndAdjustSeasoning*

How much herb is too much?

I've used a flavor meter next to each recipe, indicating the strength of the herb in the dish. One shaded leaf indicates that the herbal flavor is subtle; two indicates a prominent herbal flavor; three shaded leaves indicates a dominant herbal flavor. It's important to note that more isn't necessarily better. Some herbs become bitter if you use too much. Before you add more, try it as written and make notes.

Connect on Instagram

I'd love to hear from you! Let me know how you've found the recipes and share your inventive ways to use herbs. Find me @Gail_Herndon_Huskins.

Preserving Herbs for Year-Round Use

This book is intended to help you use up what herbs you grow or purchase, and keep you from getting bored in the process. Preserving herbs allow you to enjoy them throughout the year, well past some of their growing seasons. The key is to preserve them in some form of fat to hold their flavor. Process them together and then freeze. It's that simple. Silicone freezer trays are my preferred method to store these blends, and super handy when you want to measure out an exact amount. Here's how:

Clean herbs and dry well with a cloth. Remove any damaged leaves or stems you won't be using and discard. Decide which fat you want to use, either olive oil or non-dairy butter.

For oil
Use 2 cups herb for every 1/3 cup olive oil.

For non-dairy butter
Use ¼ cup herb for every ½ cup non-dairy butter.

Place herb and selected fat into a food processor and process until smooth. Store in silicone freezer trays in 1 or 2 tablespoon portions. Mixture will keep about 6 months.

Note: this is not recommended nor necessary for lavender.

If you have time, you can dry herbs in the refrigerator. Wash and completely dry herbs and place in a single layer on a flexible cutting mat or rimmed baking sheet. Set in the refrigerator undisturbed for 2 weeks to completely dry out.

LAVANDULA ANGUSTIFOLIA: LAVENDER

Growing Tips

Lavender is a perennial herb that thrives with at least 6 hours of sun a day and well-draining soil. It doesn't grow well indoors, but it's happy in containers on a porch or patio.

Harvest leaves and flowers early in the morning, when the fragrance is fresh. To cut flowers alone, cut stems just above the top leaves.

When dried, all parts of the lavender plant can be used as fire starter.

To give your soil a boost, grind up any unused stems, flowers, and leaves and mix into the dirt.

The plant tends to get woody after five years, so plan to replace it then.

Varieties

With over 200 varieties and numerous colors, why not grow more than one? Growing your own also ensures you won't be eating any pesticides. If you buy from a farm or nursery, be sure to ask how the lavender was grown and treated. Here are some of my favorites with their bud colors:

English Lavender *(Lavandula angustifolia)* is the most popular species with over 40 varieties. It's the hardiest of the species, which make it good for cold climates, and it's the best for cooking.

- *Betty's Blue (deep blue)*
- *Folgate (periwinkle-blue)*
- *Hidcote (dark purple)*
- *Hidcote Pink (rosy pink)*
- *Jean Davis (pinkish-white)*
- *Melissa (pale lavender)*
- *Munstead (intense blue)*
- *Nana Alba (white)*
- *Royal Velvet (dark purple)*

Check out **English lavender hybrids** *(Lavandula lavandin): Provence* is particularly nice.

French Lavender *(Lavandula dentate)* thrives in warm climates and blooms almost continually though it is not as fragrant as others. The flowers are the most intense purple color.

- *Dusky Maiden (pale purple)*
- *Goodwin Creek Grey (deep blue)*
- *Ploughman's Blue (dark blue)*

Spanish Lavender (*Lavandula stoechas*): This variety is easily distinguished from others because of its pineapple-shaped flower head. The flavor also differs in that it's spicy, making it good for more savory dishes. Not your usual tranquilizing lavender, Spanish lavender has a simulating effect. It blooms almost continuously from mid spring to late summer.

- *Ballerina (purple flowers, white bracts)*

- *Curly Top (purple flowers, fuchsia bracts)*

- *Hazel (blue-purple)*

- *Kew Red (medium to dark pink)*

- *Otto Quast (medium purple)*

- *Tickled Pink (rosy pink)*

Spike/Dutch Lavender (*Lavandula latifolia*): Similar to English lavender in appearance, but with broader leaves and frequently branching flower stalks. The scent hints of spice and camphor.

Cooking Tips

Store dried lavender in a tightly covered container in a dry space. The potency will increase with drying and should keep up to a year.

Remove the smell of onions or garlic from your hands by rubbing a few fresh lavender stalks between your fingers.

Recipes may refer to lavender flowers as buds. Flowers or buds and leaves can be used interchangeably, but sometimes the color of the flowers makes a recipe pop. Choose accordingly.

If you make your own Herbs de Provence, add lavender into the mix.

Lavender Garlic Butter

Lavender-Infused Truffles with Pistachios

Lavender Orange French Toast with Orange Maple Syrup

Lavender, Pineapple and Macadamia Muffins

Land Scallops with Lavender

Cool Cantaloupe Soup with Lavender

Lavender, Apricot and Currant Scones

Chocolate-Black Bean Bronuts with Lavender

Red Cabbage with Lavender

Lavender Shortbread

Lavender Lemonade

@Gail_Herndon_Huskins

Blueberry, Lavender and Champagne Sorbet

Toasted Macadamias with Lavender Sugar

Champagne Mango & Cucumber Salad with Lavender

LAVENDER RECIPES

Substitute 1 tablespoon fresh for every teaspoon dried

Lavender pairs well with apple, apricot, avocado, beans, beets, blueberries, cabbage, cantaloupe, capers, cherries, chocolate, coconut, corn, eggplant, garlic, hearts of palm, lemon, macadamia nuts, mango, mushroom, olives, onions, oranges, pasta, peaches, pineapple, potato, rice, strawberries and tomatoes.

Lavender, Cherry and Coconut Granola

Make granola once and you'll never buy store-bought again. It's a straight-forward process, and easily customized with your favorite canned fruit, nuts and seeds. Canned mandarin oranges are another good combo with lavender.

Makes 4 cups.

2 tablespoons dried lavender, buds and leaves
1 cup old-fashioned oats
¾ cup spelt flour
¾ cup packed brown sugar
½ teaspoon baking powder
¼ teaspoon baking soda
6 tablespoons non-dairy butter
¼ cup slivered or sliced almonds
One 14.5-ounce can tart cherries in water, drained well
2 teaspoons fresh lemon zest
2 tablespoons pumpkin seeds
2 tablespoons unsweetened shredded coconut

Preheat oven to 350°F. Grind lavender in a spice grinder and set aside.

In a large bowl, combine oats, flour, sugar, baking powder, soda and ground lavender and mix well to break up the sugar. Use a fork to cut non-dairy butter into flour, forming coarse crumbs. Stir in almonds. Press mixture into the bottom of an ungreased 9-by-12-inch baking pan, smoothing the top. Bake 12 minutes. Remove from oven and stir well. Press mixture into the bottom of pan and bake 5 more minutes.

Place cherries in a medium bowl and squeeze to extract any remaining liquid. Discard. Mix in zest. Spread on top of baked mixture and sprinkle with pumpkin seeds and coconut.

Place in oven and bake 20 minutes, or until fruit has dried and mix is golden brown. Cool completely before breaking into clusters. Store refrigerated in an air-tight container.

Vegetable Pasta with Lavender

If you need an introduction to cooking or eating lavender, this is a good first recipe. There are no other "surprise" ingredients and the taste shows you just how pleasing lavender can be in a savory dish.
Makes 8-10 servings.

13.25 ounces small, textured pasta (campanelle, fusilli, bow-tie or orecchiette)
1 tablespoon organic, cold-pressed, unrefined coconut oil
2 cups broccoli florets
1 red onion, quartered and thinly sliced
1 leek, white and light green parts, halved lengthwise, and thinly sliced
1 fennel bulb, halved lengthwise, cored and thinly sliced
1½ tablespoons dried lavender flowers and/or leaves
1 tablespoon minced fresh garlic
1 teaspoon sea salt
½ teaspoon black pepper
½ cup Greek olives, minced

Cook pasta according directions. Meanwhile, bring a large sauté pan to medium heat. When warm, add oil to coat the bottom. Add broccoli, onion, leek, fennel, lavender, crushing between your fingers as you add, garlic, salt and pepper. Stir well to mix. Cover and cook 8-10 minutes, or until vegetables are cooked through but not soft, stirring halfway through to cook evenly. Taste and adjust seasoning. Turn off heat, add olives and stir to incorporate.

Drain pasta well and add to a large bowl. Add vegetables and stir well to incorporate. Taste and adjust seasoning. Serve warm.

Lavender Lemonade

This is my go-to, non-alcoholic summer beverage. Mix with ice tea for a Lavender Lady Arnold Palmer. #MightBeGoodWithBourbon
Makes ~9 cups, 8 servings.

6 cups water
2½ cups sugar
3½ tablespoons dried lavender buds
2 cups fresh lemon juice
1 cup fresh lime juice
Lemon slices to garnish
Lavender stalks, to garnish

In a large saucepan, bring 3 cups water and sugar to a boil. Reduce to a simmer and stir until sugar is dissolved. Remove from heat and add lavender, crushing between your fingers as you add. Cool to room temperature.

Use a fine-mesh strainer to strain out the lavender, using a wooden spoon to extract as much flavor as possible. Discard lavender. Cover and refrigerate until chilled.

Place remaining 3 cups water in a large pitcher along with chilled lavender syrup, lemon and lime juices and stir well. Pour into ice-filled glasses, garnished with lemon wedges and lavender stalks.

Land Scallops with Lavender

I've tried a few substitutes for scallops and hearts of palm are just one of the good ones. For a more authentic "sea" flavor, add a ½ teaspoon kelp granules to the salt mixture. #It'sJustFun2SayLandScallops
Makes 6-8 servings.

One 25-ounce jar large hearts of palm
½ teaspoon salt
½ teaspoon black pepper
A pinch cayenne
2 tablespoons organic, cold-pressed, unrefined coconut oil, divided
4 medium shallots, minced
2 cloves garlic, minced
8 ounces cremini mushrooms, cleaned and rough chopped
1 teaspoon Herbs de Provence
1 teaspoon dried lavender flowers, leaves or a mixture
One 28-ounce can peeled and diced Italian plum tomatoes
1/4 cup dry white wine (Sauvignon Blanc, Pinot Gris, Pinot Blanc)

Drain hearts of palm and lay on a paper towel to soak up any liquid. Slice into 1" pieces.

In a small bowl, combine salt, pepper and cayenne. Season tops of cut hearts of palm with half the mixture and set aside.

Bring a large frying pan to medium-high heat and add 1½ tablespoon oil. Add hearts of palm, seasoned side down. Season tops with remaining salt mixture. Sear until lightly browned, about 3 minutes per side. It won't hurt to cook them long and get a little char on them. Remove from pan and set aside.

Lightly wipe the frying pan with a paper towel. Bring to medium heat and add remaining oil, shallots and garlic. Stir continuously and cook until translucent. Add mushrooms, Herbs de Provence and lavender, crushing between your fingertips as you add. Stir continuously until mushrooms are soft and have released their juices. Add tomatoes and wine and stir to mix well. Lower heat and simmer 10 minutes. Taste and adjust seasoning.

Place "scallops" back in the pan and cook ~5 minutes, or until heated throughout. Serve warm over rice, pasta or a bed of raw baby spinach.

New Potatoes with Red Onion and Lavender

This is one of my favorite recipes to showcase lavender. Blend with a stick blender if you prefer creamy potatoes, and if you're a butter lover, finish with non-dairy butter in place of the vinegar. #LavenderAromatherapy Makes 8-10 servings.

20 red new potatoes, scrubbed clean
2 tablespoons non-dairy butter
4 medium red onions, thinly sliced
1 tablespoon dried lavender flowers, leaves or a mixture
¼ teaspoon sea salt
Freshly ground black pepper
3 tablespoons balsamic vinegar, to garnish

Grind lavender in a spice grinder and set aside. Bring a large stockpot of salted water to a boil. Add potatoes, reduce heat to a simmer and cook 15 minutes, until fork-tender. Remove to a plate to cool.

Bring a large frying pan to medium-low heat. Add non-dairy butter, onions and a pinch salt. Cover and cook 5 minutes. Stir to break up onions, cover and cook another 15 minutes, stirring occasionally.

While onions are cooking, cut potatoes into sixths or equal size chunks. Add to onions and ground lavender. Stir to incorporate, cover and cook 5 minutes.

Remove from heat. Taste and adjust seasoning. Drizzle with balsamic vinegar and serve.

Lavender Jelly

The heavenly aroma and rose color make this a welcomed addition to breakfast toast, stirred into carbonated water, or on top of vegan angel food cake.
Makes 2 cups.

1 cup dry white wine (Sauvignon Blanc or Pinot Gris)
1 cup apple cider or unsweetened apple juice
¼ cup black currant jam
¼ cup sugar
2 tablespoons lemon juice
2 tablespoons dried lavender flowers
4 tablespoons water
4 teaspoons agar-agar powder or 4 tablespoons agar-agar flakes

Add wine, cider, jam and sugar to a medium sauce pan and gently heat, stirring to melt sugar and break up jam. Remove from heat and stir in lemon juice.

Place lavender in a small bowl, crushing between your fingers as you add. Pour warmed wine mixture over lavender, cover and infuse 10 minutes.

In a small bowl, combine water and agar-agar and stir to mix well. Add to a small saucepan with lavender infusion and bring to a boil. Lower heat and simmer 3 minutes. Use a fine-mesh strainer to remove solids, pressing on the lavender with a wooden spoon to extract as much flavor as possible.

Transfer to a clean jar and cool completely before sealing. Jelly will set up as it cools. Store in refrigerator and use within 2 weeks.

Lavender Garlic Butter

Grinding the lavender with a mortar and pestle helps diffuse the flavor throughout the butter. Sprinkle a few, really just a few, dark purple buds on top for color.
Makes ½ cup.

½ cup non-dairy butter, (1 stick) softened to room temperature
¼ teaspoon minced garlic
1 tablespoon minced chives
½ tablespoon minced parsley
¾ teaspoon dried lavender buds, ground in a mortar and pestle
¼ teaspoon white pepper

Combine all ingredients in a small bowl and mix well with a fork. Taste and adjust seasoning, keeping in mind the flavors will meld more as it sets. Cover and keep refrigerator. Use within 2 weeks.

Lavender Extract

Bump up the lavender flavor in baked goods by using this in place of vanilla extract. #MakesANiceGiftToo
Makes 2 cups.

1/4 cup dried lavender flowers
16 ounces 100-proof vodka

Place both ingredients in a Mason jar and seal. Shake well to mix and place in a dark location for 1 week to infuse.

Use a fine-mesh strainer to strain out lavender and discard. Transfer extract to a clean Mason jar and seal tightly. Keep refrigerated and use within 6 months.

Lavender Ratatouille

This French dish combines seasonal summer vegetables, all simmered together. The addition of lavender only makes it more French. #N'est-cePas?

Makes 8-10 servings.

1 tablespoon organic, cold-pressed, unrefined coconut oil
1½ cups small diced yellow onion
4 garlic cloves, minced
1 pound eggplant, destemmed, skin intact, cut into ½" cubes
8 ounces baby bella or cremini mushrooms, rough chopped, ~3 cups
2 medium zucchini, sliced ¼" thick
2 medium summer squash, sliced ¼" thick
2 bell peppers, any color, medium diced
1½ tablespoons dried lavender flowers, leaves or a mixture
One 15-ounce can crushed plum tomatoes
½ cup fresh parsley, minced
¼ cup capers, well drained
½ teaspoon sea salt
½ teaspoon black pepper
2 tablespoons nutritional yeast, plus more for serving

Preheat oven to 375°F.

Bring the largest sauté pan you have to medium heat. Add oil, onion and garlic and sauté 5 minutes, stirring often until browned. Lower heat to a simmer and add eggplant and cover. Cook 10 minutes, stirring at the midpoint. Eggplant should be almost soft. Add mushrooms, zucchini, squash, bell peppers, and lavender, crushing between your fingertips as you add.

Return heat to medium-low. Stir well to mix, cover and cook 15 minutes, stirring occasionally.

Add tomatoes, parsley, capers, salt and pepper. Stir well to mix. Taste and adjust seasoning. Cover and cook 5 minutes.

Transfer to a 9-by-13-inch baking dish and bake 10 minutes. Remove from oven and sprinkle with nutritional yeast. Return to oven for 5 more minutes. Serve with additional nutritional yeast, if desired.

Lavender Bread with Black Olives and Chives

Don't stress when you see oatmeal flour in the ingredient list. It's easy to make your own. Place 1¼ cups oatmeal in a food processor and process until finely ground. That'll yield 1 cup of oatmeal flour.
Makes 1 loaf.

1 tablespoon flax meal
3 cups all-purpose flour
1 cup oatmeal flour
2 tablespoons sugar
2½ tablespoons dried lavender flowers, leaves or a mixture
2 teaspoons baking powder
1 teaspoon baking soda
1 teaspoon sea salt
1 teaspoon black pepper
2 cups non-dairy milk
1 teaspoon vinegar
1/3 cup rough chopped Greek olives
¼ cup minced fresh chives
¾ tablespoon quick oats

In a medium bowl, combine flax meal with 2½ tablespoons water. Mix well and set aside.

Preheat oven to 375°F. Lightly oil a 9-by-5-inch loaf pan with non-stick spray and set aside. In a large bowl, sift flour, oat flour, sugar, lavender, crushing between your fingers as you add, baking powder, soda, salt and pepper. Stir to mix well and set aside.

Add non-dairy milk and vinegar to the flax meal bowl and whisk to blend. Stir in olives and chives. Add to flour mixture and stir until just mixed. Transfer to prepared pan and sprinkle quick oats on top, gently pressing into dough. Bake 35–40 minutes, or until a knife comes out clean. Remove to a wire rack to cool before cutting.

Lavender Shortbread

These cookies are fancy in their simplicity. Using with a round cookie or biscuit cutter ensures the lavender gets all the attention. For the best visual appeal, use dark purple lavender buds.
Makes forty 2" cookies.

1 tablespoon ground flax meal
½ cup plus ½ tablespoon sugar, divided
1½ tablespoons dried lavender flowers, divided
1/8 teaspoon sea salt
1 cup non-dairy butter, cut into small chunks
2 cups all-purpose flour
4 tablespoons cornstarch

In a small bowl, mix flax meal with 2½ tablespoons water and set aside.

Line two cookie sheets with silicone mats and set aside.

In a food processor, mix ½ cup sugar with 1 tablespoon lavender for 15 seconds. Add salt and non-dairy butter and pulse until well incorporated. Add flax meal mixture and pulse again. Add flour and cornstarch and pulse until small crumbles form.

Transfer to a small bowl and cover with a damp cloth. Refrigerate 2 hours or overnight.

Roll dough out to a ¼" thickness. It will be pretty hard initially, but will warm to your hands and become softer. Cut with 2" cookie cutters and transfer to prepared baking sheets. Smooth any ragged edges with your fingers. Refrigerate 20 minutes.

Preheat oven to 325°F.

With a mortar and pestle, crush remaining ½ tablespoon sugar and remaining ½ tablespoon lavender. Set aside.

Remove cookies from the refrigerator and sprinkle each with the sugar mixture, using it all. Bake 15–20 minutes, and edges start turning golden. Cool before serving.

Lavender-Infused Strawberry Jam

Elevate any breakfast or brunch with this easy-to-make jam. It's great on scones, waffles or toast. Recycle the soaking liquid buy freezing it in mini-ice cube trays. The pretty rosy-red ice cubes add a hint of strawberry flavor to flat or sparkling water.
Makes 2 pints.

3 cups water
1½ tablespoons dried lavender flowers, leaves or a mixture
3 cups fresh strawberries, cleaned, stemmed and halved
3½ tablespoons chia seeds
2 tablespoons lemon juice
2 tablespoons light agave

To make the lavender infusion, bring water to a boil in a medium stock pot. Add lavender, crushing between your fingertips as you add. Turn off heat, cover and steep 30 minutes.

Use a fine mesh strainer to strain out lavender, pressing as much flavor as possible with the back of a wooden spoon. Discard lavender. Pour liquid into a large mixing bowl. Add strawberries, cover and refrigerate 4 hours or overnight.

Use a spider strainer to remove strawberries from liquid and process in a food processor until smooth, scraping down the sides as necessary. Reserve liquid for ice cubes or discard. Add chia seeds, lemon juice and agave and process until well incorporated. Taste and adjust seasoning. Transfer to a pint jar, seal and refrigerate. Jam will firm up in half an hour. Store in refrigerator and use within 2 weeks.

Pineapple–Lavender Vinegar

For the most color, use the deepest purple lavender buds for this infusion. The vinegar adds a surprisingly good zing to melon wedges or fresh strawberries, or use in place of white vinegar in salad dressing recipes. Makes 1 cup.

¾ tablespoon dried lavender flowers
½ cup fresh pineapple cut in ½" dice
1 cup white or champagne vinegar
¼ teaspoon sea salt

To release the essential oils, squeeze the lavender flowers with your fingers as you add them to a sterilized glass container Add pineapple, cover with vinegar and add salt. Seal tightly and shake well.

Place in a cool, dark place for 1 week and shake once a day. Strain and discard solids. Transfer to a sterilized glass jar with a tight-fitting lid and seal tightly. Store in the refrigerator and use within 2 months.

Blueberry-Lavender Crisp

A pretty basic crisp, but jazzed up with subtle hints of lavender.
#NotSoBasicAnymore
Makes 6–8 servings.

5 cups fresh or frozen blueberries
½ cup sugar plus 2 tablespoons
1 tablespoon fresh lemon juice
1 teaspoon vanilla extract
2 tablespoons dried lavender flowers, leaves or a mixture, divided
¾ cup all-purpose flour plus 2 tablespoons, divided
½ cup old-fashioned oats
1/3 cup packed brown sugar
½ teaspoon cinnamon
¼ teaspoon salt
½ cup non-dairy milk
½ cup walnuts, rough-chopped
3 tablespoons non-dairy butter

Preheat oven to 350°F. Lightly grease an 8" square baking pan with non-stick spray and set aside.

In a large bowl, mix together berries, sugar, lemon juice, extract and ½ tablespoon lavender, crushing between your fingertips as you add. Stir in 2 tablespoons flour and spoon into prepared pan. Spread evenly with a spatula, pressing into the pan.

In another bowl, combine remaining ¾ cup flour, oats, brown sugar, cinnamon, salt and remaining 1½ tablespoons lavender, crushing between your fingertips as you add. Spoon on top of berries. Pour non-dairy milk on top and sprinkle with walnuts. Cut non-dairy butter into small pieces and scatter across the top.

Bake 45 minutes, or until top is golden brown and serve warm.

Coconut Lavender Cream

This sweet cream is a decadent dessert on its own or as a topping for pudding or pie. Reserve some for Lavender French Toast, and Toasted Macadamias with Lavender Sugar, if you can.

Makes 1½ cups; 3 individual servings or 10–12 big dollops.

One13.5-ounce can coconut cream (not milk)
2 teaspoons dried lavender buds
1 tablespoon cornstarch
2 tablespoons cream de cassis, plum liqueur or brandy

In a small sauce pan, add coconut cream and lavender, crushing between your fingers as you add. Bring to a simmer for 2 minutes. Remove from heat, stir in corn starch and steep one hour uncovered.

Use a fine-mesh strainer to strain out lavender, pressing with the back of a wooden spoon to extract as much flavor from the lavender as desired. Discard lavender and stir in liqueur. Taste and adjust seasoning. Transfer to a medium mixing bowl, cover and refrigerate 30 minutes before serving. Store refrigerated in a sealed container.

To serve with Toasted Macadamias with Lavender Sugar, spoon some into shallow bowls and top with the nuts and a few lavender buds.

Toasted Macadamias with Lavender Sugar

Toasting nuts completely transforms them, making them more complex in flavor. We're taking it one step further, adding an herbal-sugar layer that changes their flavor yet again.
Makes 3 cups.

1 tablespoon organic, cold-pressed, unrefined coconut oil
½ cup granulated sugar
2 tablespoons dried lavender leaves and buds, ground in a spice grinder
3 cups raw macadamia nuts, halves or large pieces, of equal size
2 teaspoons non-dairy butter
½ teaspoon vanilla extract
¼ teaspoon sea salt

Spread coconut oil on a rimmed baking sheet and set aside.

In a food processor, process sugar with ground lavender.

Bring a large, dry frying pan to medium heat. Add nuts and stir frequently until lightly browned and fragrant. Add sugar-lavender mix and cook, stirring constantly, until sugar is melted and begins to caramelize.

Turn off heat and stir in non-dairy butter, extract and salt and mix well. Transfer nuts to prepared baking sheet to cool. Store in a sealed container in the refrigerator.

Red Cabbage with Lavender

This warm dish is very potluckable. Aside from traveling well, it holds up over time, and gives an added pop of color on the plate. #MakeAnEntrance
Makes 6½–7 cups, ~6 servings.

½ cup walnut halves or large pieces
½ medium red cabbage, cored and quartered
1 Granny Smith apple, scrubbed clean, skin intact, cored and cut into
   eights
1 tablespoon organic, cold-pressed, unrefined coconut oil
1 tablespoon minced garlic, minced
½ cup finely chopped red onion
2 tablespoons minced fresh parsley
2 tablespoons fresh lemon juice
1½ tablespoons apple cider vinegar
½ tablespoon Dijon mustard
½ teaspoon sea salt
1 tablespoon dried lavender buds, leaves or a mixture, ground in a spice
   grinder

Bring a large, dry frying pan to medium high heat. Add nuts and a pinch of both sea salt and black pepper. Stir regularly to toast. Remove from pan and set aside.

In a food processor fitted with the shredding blade, shred cabbage and apples. Transfer to a large bowl and set aside.

Wipe frying pan with a dry paper towel, removing any nut traces. Bring pan to medium heat and add oil, garlic, onion, parsley, lemon juice, vinegar, Dijon and salt. Cook 2 minutes, stirring constantly. Add cabbage, apples and lavender and stir well. Cover and cook 8–10 minutes, stirring occasionally, until warmed throughout. Taste and adjust seasoning. Transfer to a serving dish.

Rough chop toasted nuts and add to cabbage. Taste and adjust seasoning and serve warm.

Lavender Oatmeal Chocolate Chips

I don't have to twist your arm to try this recipe, do I? Cookies are an easy sell, especially the classics with a little tweak. Add ½ cup peanut butter to the batter for yet another twist. #CookieLove
Makes 4 dozen.

2 tablespoons flax meal
2/3 cup non-dairy butter, at room temperature
½ cup granulated sugar
½ cup packed brown sugar
2 teaspoons vanilla extract
2/3 cup non-dairy milk
2 cups flour
1 cup old fashioned oats
3 tablespoons dried lavender flowers, leaves or a mixture, ground in a
   spice grinder
1 teaspoon baking soda
1 teaspoon baking powder
1 teaspoon salt
1 cup rough-chopped raw walnuts
2 cups semi-sweet non-dairy chocolate chips

In a small bowl, combine flax meal with 5 tablespoons water and mix well. Set aside. Pre-heat over to 350°F.

In a medium mixing bowl, cream non-dairy butter with sugars. Add vanilla and non-dairy milk and stir well. Add flax meal mixture and mix well to combine.

Preheat oven to 400°F.

Line a cookie sheet with parchment paper and set aside.

In a large mixing bowl, combine flour, oats, sugar, baking powder, baking soda, salt and ground lavender. Add non-dairy butter, cutting it into the flour with a fork. Mix until it has the consistency of coarse meal.

Make a well in the center of the flour. Stir in applesauce, extract and non-dairy milk-vinegar mixture, forming a soft dough. Gently fold in pecans, apricots and currants, being careful not to overwork the flour.

Form dough into a 1-inch high circle and place on prepared cookie sheet. Cut into 8 wedges but don't slice all the way through to separate. Bake 15 minutes, or until lightly browned and a toothpick inserted into the center comes out clean. Serve warm.

Tropical Lavender Rice

Cooking rice in coconut cream gives it the consistency of sticky rice. After all, you've got two of the primary ingredients. For a nice presentation, use a ramekin, small cup or donut mold to create uniform rice mounds. #PlatingTip

Makes 3 cups, ~4 servings.

1 tablespoon organic, cold-pressed, unrefined coconut oil
1 cup finely chopped yellow or red onion
1 tablespoon freshly grated ginger root
2 teaspoons freshly minced garlic
1 cup uncooked jasmine rice
1½ cups vegetable broth
1 cup coconut cream
¼ teaspoon sea salt
¾ cup fresh chopped or canned crushed pineapple, well drained
½ cup parsley, finely chopped
2 tablespoons minced chives
1 tablespoon soy sauce
1 tablespoon dried lavender flowers, leaves or a mixture, ground in a spice grinder
½ tablespoon lemon zest
½ tablespoon lime zest
Freshly ground black pepper

Bring a medium saucepan to medium-high heat. Add oil and onions and sauté 4-5 minutes stirring regularly, until softened. Add ginger and garlic and cook 1 minute. Add rice, broth, cream and salt and bring to a low boil.

Reduce heat to medium-low, cover and cook 10 minutes. Stir well to keep it from sticking to the bottom. Cover and cook 10 more minutes or until rice is cooked and liquid is absorbed.

Remove from heat and stir in pineapple, parsley, chives, soy sauce, ground lavender, lemon and lime zests and black pepper. Stir to mix well, then cover and let stand 5 minutes. Taste and adjust seasoning. Serve warm.

Lavender-Orange French Toast

Lightly adapted from Judi and Jim Brady's Lavender Cuisine. This makes any breakfast a special occasion. #AKAWeekends
Makes 8 slices, 3-4 servings.

1½ cups freshly squeezed orange juice
¾ cup soft tofu
1½ teaspoons dried lavender flowers, leaves or a mixture
Eight 1" thick slices of French bread
½ cup maple syrup
1 tablespoon Curaçao or Triple Sec
Coconut Lavender Cream, optional

In a high-speed blender, process 1 cup orange juice and tofu until well blended. Set aside.

Crush lavender with a mortar and pestle and add to blender with orange juice. Process to incorporate. Pour into an 8-by-12-inch baking pan. Place bread in batter and turn to coat both sides.

Bring a dry, medium-size skillet to medium-high heat. When hot, lower heat to medium and lightly coat pan with non-stick cooking spray. Fry bread 2½-3 minutes per side, until golden brown. Transfer to a plate and cover to keep warm.

In a small saucepan, heat maple syrup with remaining ½ cup orange juice and liqueur. Serve warm over French toast, topped with Coconut Lavender Cream, if desired.

Cool Cantaloupe Soup with Lavender

Lightly adapted from Sharon Shipley's The Lavender Cookbook. Combat the intense heat of summer by eating cold soup, though just looking at this pale orange soup will help. #EatCool2StayCool
Makes 8 cups; 6-8 servings.

2 ripe oranges
2¼ cups cubed cantaloupe
1 pound frozen peaches
¼ cup lime juice
½ tablespoon agave
½ cup sweet white wine (Riesling or Gewurztraminer)
2 tablespoons non-dairy vanilla yogurt
1½ teaspoons dried lavender, ground with a mortar and pestle
1 tablespoon dried dark purple lavender buds, to garnish
Coconut Lavender Cream to garnish, if desired

Juice oranges and transfer juice to a high-speed blender. Add cantaloupe chunks, peaches, lime juice, agave, wine, non-dairy yogurt and lavender. Process until smooth. Taste and adjust seasoning. Cover and refrigerate at least 3 hours or overnight.

Ladle cold soup into chilled bowls and garnish with a swirl of Coconut Lavender Cream and a pinch lavender buds.

Chocolate-Black Bean Bronuts with Lavender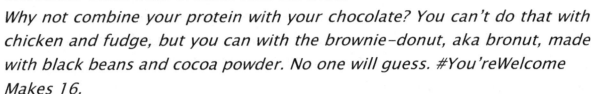

Why not combine your protein with your chocolate? You can't do that with chicken and fudge, but you can with the brownie-donut, aka bronut, made with black beans and cocoa powder. No one will guess. #You'reWelcome Makes 16.

2 tablespoons ground flax meal
2½ teaspoons dried lavender flowers, leaves or a mixture
Two 15.25-ounce cans black beans, rinsed and well drained (3 cups)
¾ cup plus 2 tablespoons Dutch-process cocoa powder
1 cup old-fashioned oats
1½ teaspoons baking powder
½ teaspoon salt
½ teaspoon instant coffee powder
1 cup maple syrup
2 teaspoons vanilla or lavender extract
2/3 cup organic, cold-pressed, unrefined coconut oil, melted
1/3 cup non-dairy mini-chocolate chips
¾ tablespoon dried, dark purple lavender buds to garnish

In a small bowl, mix flax meal with 5 tablespoons water and set aside.

Preheat oven to 350°F. Grease two 8-donut mold pans lightly with non-stick spray and set aside.

Grind lavender in a mortar and pestle and set aside.

In a food processor, combine beans, cocoa, oats, ground lavender, baking powder, salt, and instant coffee powder and process until well mixed. Add maple syrup, vanilla, flax mixture and oil and process again until well incorporated. Fold in chocolate chips.

Pour mixture in prepared pans and sprinkle with dark purple lavender buds. Bake 20-25 minutes, or when a cake tester inserted into the center comes out clean. Cool completely before removing from pan.

Lavender–Peach BBQ Sauce

Adapted from Judi and Jim Brady's Lavender Cuisine. This is easy, quick and delicious, not to mention another unexpected use of culinary lavender. Continuing with the unexpected, try some as a base for homemade pizza, stirred into mashed potatoes, or as a marinade for grilled veggie burgers. #AsIfLavenderBBQSauceWasn'tUnexpectedEnough
Makes 3½ cups.

1 cup peach preserves
1 cup small dice yellow onion
1 cup organic ketchup
¼ cup packed brown sugar
¼ cup vegan Worcestershire sauce
¼ cup apple cider vinegar
1 tablespoon dried lavender flowers, leaves or a mixture, ground in a spice grinder
1 teaspoon powdered mustard
1 teaspoon sweet (Hungarian) paprika
¼ teaspoon hot sauce

In a medium saucepan over medium–low heat, combine all ingredients and bring to a boil. Reduce heat and simmer, stirring occasionally until slightly thickened, ~10–15 minutes. Taste and adjust seasoning. Cool before sealing in a 2-pint Mason jar and store in the refrigerator.

Beet and Bean Salad with Lavender

I thought this standard vegetable combo could benefit from a little refresh. Lavender to the rescue.
Makes 8 servings.

1 pound tender green beans, washed and ends trimmed
1 pound tender yellow beans, washed and ends trimmed
¾ cup hemp oil, *No-Oil Oil* (in Basics), or extra virgin olive oil
½ cup red wine vinegar
1½ tablespoons dried lavender flowers, leaves or a mixture
2 teaspoons freshly minced garlic
1 teaspoon sea salt
½ teaspoon freshly ground black pepper
8 small cooked beets, quartered
1 cup minced shallots
¼ cup chopped chives
Zest of 1 small lemon

Bring a large stockpot of salted water to a boil. Add beans and cook 5-6 minutes, or until tender yet still crunchy to the bite. Use a spider strainer to transfer beans into an ice bath. Drain well and set aside.

In a large serving bowl, whisk together oil, vinegar, lavender, crushing between your fingers as you add, garlic, salt and pepper. Taste and adjust seasoning.

Add cooled beans, beets, shallots, and chives to the bowl with the dressing and toss well to cover. Refrigerate 20 minutes to allow flavors to meld. Top with lemon zest before serving.

Crostini with Lavender Tapenade

My mouth is watering just writing the ingredient list. I can imagine the aroma as well as the first bite: an initial crunch of the toasted bread, and then the crazy zing of garlic, capers, olives and lemon, the smoothness of the mushrooms, and the lavender weaving it all together. If you find your body responding to something you're reading, that's a good sign. #MightBeFromHeaven

Makes ~2½ cups.

½ cup capers, well drained

4 cups sliced cremini or baby bella mushrooms

½ cup pitted Greek olives, packed and well drained

2 teaspoons white truffle oil, extra-virgin olive oil or *No-Oil Oil* (in Basics)

2 small garlic cloves

2 teaspoons fresh lemon juice

1/3 cup fresh parsley plus ½ cup to garnish

2 teaspoons dried lavender leaves, flowers or a mixture, ground in a spice grinder

1 teaspoon black pepper

1 French baguette, cut into ¼–½" slices on the diagonal

In a food processor, combine capers, mushrooms, olives, oil, garlic, lemon juice, 1/3 cup parsley, ground lavender and pepper until smooth, scraping down the sides as needed. Taste and adjust seasoning. Transfer to a medium serving bowl and set aside.

Preheat oven to 400°F. Place bread slices on an ungreased baking sheet and place on the middle rack. Toast until browned to your liking, turning to toast both sides. Remove from oven and transfer to a large serving tray. Spread with tapenade and garnish with reserved ½ cup parsley. Serve immediately.

Lavender, Pineapple and Macadamia Muffins

Sounds like a tropical vacation, doesn't it? All that's missing is the sunscreen. These turn out moist and tender, with a couple of sweet things to chew on, literally. #Staycation
Makes one dozen.

¾ cup raw, unsalted macadamia nuts
½ cup plus 2 tablespoons pineapple juice
1 large ripe banana
3/4 cup sugar
1½ cups spelt flour
½ cup oats
½ cup oat bran
1½ teaspoons baking soda
1½ teaspoons baking powder
½ teaspoon salt
½ teaspoon allspice
¾ tablespoon plus 2 teaspoons dried lavender flowers, divided

Bring a dry, medium frying pan to medium heat. Add macadamia nuts and stir to toast constantly, 1½–2 minutes. Remove from pan and set aside to cool.

Preheat oven to 400°F. Grease a 12-cup muffin tin with non-stick spray and set aside.

In a large mixing bowl, use a stick blender to combine pineapple juice and banana. Add sugar and mix until smooth.

Rough chop macadamia nuts and set aside.

In a separate bowl, combine flour, oats, oat bran, baking soda, baking powder, salt, allspice and 2 teaspoons lavender, ground with a mortar and pestle. Mix well. Stir in nuts. Fold flour mixture into wet ingredients until just mixed.

Fill muffin cups halfway full and top with remaining ¾ tablespoon lavender divided between the muffins. Bake 12 minutes or until a toothpick stuck into the middle comes out clean. Cool 2 minutes in the pan before removing to a wire rack. Serve warm.

Champagne Mango and Cucumber Salad with Lavender

Because ripe mangos are so juicy, they can stretch the seasoned oil in this dressing, making a little go a long way. Use a bright purple lavender for a better contrast of colors, against the golden mango and greens of the cucumber, jalapeño and parsley. This salad is best eaten fresh.
Makes 3½ cups, 4-6 servings.

3 champagne mangos
1 Persian or Kirby cucumber
2½ tablespoons minced red onion
2 radishes, thinly sliced
2 tablespoons minced jalapeño
¼ cup fresh minced parsley
1½ teaspoons dried lavender buds, divided
½ tablespoon extra-virgin olive oil or *No-Oil Oil* (in Basics)
½ tablespoon fresh lime juice
¾ teaspoon sugar
1/8 teaspoon sea salt
Freshly ground black pepper

De-seed mangos and cut into ¾" pieces. (If you haven't cut a mango before, YouTube can help.) Place in a medium mixing bowl and set aside.

Slice cucumber thinly and quarter the slices. Add to mango along with red onion, radish, jalapeño and parsley and set aside.

In a mortar and pestle, grind 1 teaspoon lavender and set aside.

In a small bowl, combine oil, lime juice, sugar, the ground lavender, salt and black pepper. Mix well with a fork and add to mangos. Stir gently to incorporate. Taste and adjust seasoning. Sprinkle with remaining ½ teaspoon lavender. Serve atop a bed of baby spinach.

Lavender-Infused Truffles with Pistachios

Lavender is infused into the coconut cream for these truffles, creating a soft hint of the herb on the palate. #ChocolateIsMyFavoriteFoodGroup Makes ~40.

14 ounces semisweet chocolate
Coconut oil, to oil pan
1 cup canned coconut cream (not coconut milk)
½ cup sugar
3 tablespoons dried lavender flowers
½ teaspoon lavender or vanilla extract
½ cup finely chopped pistachios

Chop chocolate into small pieces and place in a metal bowl. Set aside.

Coat bottom and sides of an 8-by-8-inch baking pan with coconut oil and set aside.

Place coconut cream, sugar, lavender and extract in a small saucepan and bring to low heat. Bring to a boil, remove from heat, cover and let stand 20 minutes.

Use a fine-mesh strainer to strain out lavender, pressing with a wooden spoon to extract as much flavor as possible. Discard lavender. Gently reheat mixture, being careful not to boil. Once heated, pour over chopped chocolate. Stir to melt chocolate completely.

Pour into prepared pan and place in freezer for 10 minutes. Cut into 1" pieces and roll into balls. Place balls back into pan and refrigerate 10 minutes.

Place chopped pistachios on a medium plate. Remove truffles from refrigerator and roll in the nuts, fully coating. Serve immediately or refrigerate until ready to serve. Store refrigerated in an airtight container.

Slow-Cooked Lavender Apples with Puff Pastry

My grandmother, Dahlie, used to make fried apples for breakfast. It was a simple recipe: apples, butter and brown sugar. They cooked down for a long time on the stovetop and smelled like heaven. It goes without saying that they were delicious. For my spin, the butter is infused with lavender and a little puff pastry is thrown on top. I make it for breakfast but it could pass for dessert. #RecipeHeirloom
Makes 6-10 servings.

10 tablespoons non-dairy butter
½ cup dried lavender, plus 3-5 stalks to garnish
6 firm Granny Smith or Golden Delicious apples, peeled, cored and thinly
  sliced
½ cup packed light brown sugar
One sheet frozen puff pastry, thawed and refrigerated

Melt non-dairy butter in a small saucepan over medium-low heat. Remove from heat, add lavender, cover and set aside to infuse 30 minutes.

Warm butter again and then strain through a fine-mesh sieve, pressing lavender with the back of a wooden spoon to extract as much flavor as possible. Discard lavender.

In a large cast iron skillet, arrange apple slices in a swirl, starting in the middle and working your way out, with slices facing the same direction. Pour infused butter on top, then sprinkle with brown sugar. Cover and cook over medium-low heat for 1 hour, without stirring. Apples will be browned on the bottom and halfway cooked. Cool 30 minutes.

Meanwhile, heat oven to 400°F. Cover apples with the puff pastry, being careful not to stretch or tear it. Use kitchen shears to trim off the corners, and press the pastry lightly around the inside edge of the pan, covering the apples. Poke five or more vent holes in the center with a sharp knife.

Place in oven and bake 15 minutes, or until golden brown all over. Cool 10 minutes before garnishing with lavender stalks. Slice and serve warm.

Blueberry, Lavender and Champagne Sorbet

I love a few things about this recipe - the deep purple color, the play of lavender and blueberries together, and the fact that someone's got to finish the rest of the champagne bottle. Another thing to love? Thanks to the alcohol, there's no waiting to serve when it comes out of the freezer.
#ChampagneSmiles
Makes 3 cups, or ~4 servings.

1 cup sugar
1 cup water
2 tablespoons dried lavender flowers, leaves or a mixture
2¼ cups fresh blueberries, divided
2 tablespoons fresh lemon juice
¾ cup champagne

In a small saucepan, bring water and sugar to a boil, stirring continuously until sugar is completely dissolved. Remove from heat and add lavender, crushing between your fingertips as you add, and cover. Infuse 30 minutes.

Use a fine-mesh strainer to remove the lavender, pressing with a wooden spoon to extract as much flavor as possible. Discard lavender.

Transfer infusion to a high-speed blender and add 2 cups blueberries and lemon juice. Process until well blended. Set a fine-mesh strainer over a large bowl and press the mixture through. Discard any blueberry pulp and lavender.

Whisk in champagne. Pour into a freezer-safe container and seal. Freeze until ready to serve. Top each portion with reserved blueberries.

OCIMUM BASILICUM: BASIL

Growing Tips

Basil, especially *Sweet basil* and *Genoese* or *Italian basil*, is one of the most popular annual herbs and is easy to grow.

Basil tends to cross-pollinate, so plant different varieties separately, with lots of space between.

Grow in containers or plant in the ground where it can get lots of direct sun.

Remove flowers as they start to bud to keep the plant from going to seed.

To harvest, cut an entire branch just above a lower set of leaves. The plant will branch at that point, and grow bushier with more leaves.

Hold the stem of the plant when cutting fresh leaves, to keep them from bruising and turning brown.

Varieties

With over 150 basil varieties grown all over the world, a good nursery might stock a dozen or so of the most popular ones. Mail-order catalogues might expose you to even more. (I find it hard to resist the dark purple varieties.) I discovered Hudson Valley Seed Company at the annual Philadelphia Flower Show. (theflowershow.com) Their seed packets are little works of art. Some of my favorite varieties (not all at Hudson Valley Seed Co.):

Holy basil or *Sacred basil* is known as *tulsi* in India, where it's used medicinally and for making tea. It's very aromatic and both smells and tastes peppery. Cooking softens the flavor; you'll find it bitter if eaten raw.

Genovese aka *Italian basil* is a variety of Sweet Basil with large, flat, pointed leaves. It makes a nice substitute for lettuce in sandwiches and wraps.

Mammoth, with its super-large leaf, is great to wrap food in and cook on the grill.

Lemon basil is a wonderfully fragrant variety, good for vinegars, baked goods, salads, grain dishes and teas, not to mention for making pesto.

Lettuce leaf is another kind of Sweet Basil, with large, distinctly ruffled soft leaves.

Opal basil is a less sweet tasting variety with purple-black leaves and pink flowers. It tastes a little more like anise.

Purple Ruffles has dark shiny leaves with ruffled edges and a strong flavor.

Sweet basil is one of the most common, used in pesto and other Italian dishes.

Thai basil is frequently used in Asian cuisine, with its peppery scent and anise flavor. It can withstand the heat from cooking a bit better than others.

Noteworthy varieties
Cinnamon and *clove basil* are interesting options, and good in baked goods and bean dishes.

Lime basil is very aromatic and good in teas, salads and baked goods.

Cooking Tips
When adding basil to a finished dish, handle as little as possible to prevent discoloration.

Both the flowers and stems of basil are edible. Though not as fragrant or tasty, stems can substitute for any shortage of basil leaves in recipes.

Flowers have a stronger flavor than stems and are a nice addition to green salads. Pinch any leggy flower tops into several pieces and scatter on top.

Spicy Basil Mayo

Lentil and Veggie Basil Loaf

@Gail_Herndon_Huskins

No-Oil Basil Pesto

Basil-Infused Orange Granita

Raw Chocolate and Basil Truffles

Gluten-Free Zucchini Basil Muffins

Dreamy Basil Dressing

Wild Rice, Quinoa and Basil Pilaf

Baked Pineapple with Basil and Peanuts

Basil-Orange Butter

Watermelon Salad with Watermelon-Basil Vinaigrette

BASIL RECIPES

Substitute 1 teaspoon dried basil for every tablespoon fresh

Basil pairs well with apples, artichoke, beans, blueberries, cantaloupe, chocolate, corn, cucumber, eggplant, fennel, green beans, honey, lemon, lentils, lime, mushrooms, oranges, peppers, pecans, pineapple, pomegranate, potatoes, quinoa, spinach, split peas, tomatoes, watermelon, wild rice and zucchini.

Sweet Basil Jelly

This green jelly makes a dramatic topping on non-dairy vanilla ice cream or lemon bread, or when a tablespoon or more is added to iced tea, lemonade or sparkling water.
Makes ~3½ cups.

3¼ cups sugar
1 cup water
½ cup white vinegar
½ cup lightly packed basil leaves
3 ounces liquid fruit pectin
4 or more drops natural green food coloring, optional

In a large stockpot, combine sugar, water, vinegar and basil. Bring to a hard boil for 1 minute, stirring constantly. Remove from heat.

Use a fine-mesh strainer set up over a bowl to strain off the basil, pressing with the back of a wooden spoon to extract as much flavor as possible. Discard basil. Transfer infusion back to stockpot.

Add pectin and return to heat, boiling hard for one minute. Add food coloring, if using. Skim off foam, pour into 4 hot, sterilized, half pint jars and seal. Store in the refrigerator and use within 3 months.

Spicy Cucumber Salad with Basil

I love this combo of flavors – clean, fresh, a little sweet and a little spicy. Makes 4 cups.

3 cups sliced cucumber, thinly cut with a mandoline
½ teaspoon sea salt
½ red and ½ yellow bell pepper, diced
¼ cup plus 2 tablespoons thinly sliced scallions, white and green parts
¼ cup packed basil, minced, plus 2 tablespoons chiffonade to garnish
1–2 tablespoons seeded and minced fresh jalapeño
1½ teaspoons minced fresh garlic
1 teaspoon freshly grated ginger
½ teaspoon red pepper flakes
1 tablespoon rice wine vinegar
1 tablespoon fresh lime juice
2 tablespoons agave
1 teaspoon soy sauce
3 tablespoons coarsely chopped peanuts
Black sesame seeds, to garnish

In a large bowl, mix cucumber and salt. set aside 30 minutes.

Drain well and add bell peppers, scallions, basil, jalapeño, garlic, ginger, and red pepper flakes. Set aside.

In a small bowl, whisk together rice wine vinegar, lime juice, agave and soy sauce. Taste and adjust seasoning. Pour dressing over cucumber mixture and chill until ready to serve, at least 20 minutes.

Garnish with peanuts, basil chiffonade and black sesame seeds.

Tomato–Basil Soup with Basil Cream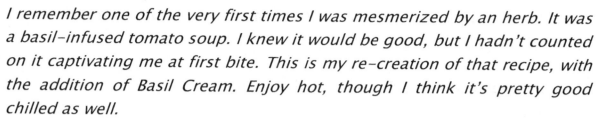

I remember one of the very first times I was mesmerized by an herb. It was a basil-infused tomato soup. I knew it would be good, but I hadn't counted on it captivating me at first bite. This is my re-creation of that recipe, with the addition of Basil Cream. Enjoy hot, though I think it's pretty good chilled as well.

Makes 5 cups; ~4 servings.

Basil Cream
¾ cup canned full fat coconut milk
½ cup packed fresh basil
1 tablespoon corn starch
1 teaspoon fresh lemon juice
½ teaspoon freshly grated lemon zest

Soup
Two 28-ounce cans whole tomatoes
¾ tablespoon organic, cold-pressed, unrefined coconut oil
½ cup small dice yellow onion
½ cup small dice carrot
½ cup small dice celery
2 teaspoons minced fresh garlic
2 cups vegetable stock
1 cup packed whole basil leaves and stems, plus more to garnish
½ teaspoon sea salt
½ teaspoon black pepper

For the basil cream, process coconut milk, basil, corn starch, lemon juice and zest with a stick blender in a small container until smooth. Taste and adjust seasoning. Transfer to a squeeze bottle and refrigerate until using.

Drain tomatoes, reserving juice from one can. Freeze juice from second can for another purpose. Over a bowl, use your fingers to break the tomatoes into smaller pieces, and separate out the seeds. Discard seeds. Set aside.

Bring a large sauté pan to medium heat. Add oil, onion, carrot and celery and cook 5 minutes, or until softened. Add garlic, tomatoes and juice, stock, basil, salt and pepper. Bring to a boil; reduce heat to medium-low and simmer 10 minutes, stirring occasionally.

Use a fork to lift out the basil and place in a fine-mesh strainer. Use the back of a wooden spoon to press on the basil, extracting as much flavor as possible. Discard. Transfer soup to a high-speed blender and purée. Taste and adjust seasoning. Pour into bowls and top with generous swirls of basil cream and basil chiffonade, if desired.

No-Oil Pesto

A no oil pesto that tastes good? Oh yeah! This is lively on grilled veggies, raw tomato slices, or as a sandwich spread (with eggplant bacon, it's yummers). Use in place of tomato sauce on homemade pizza, (like the Potato Pesto Pizza), or on your favorite pasta or gnocchi. Reserve ¼ cup to use in the Fennel, Tomato and Basil Casserole recipe. Double the recipe to have enough to play with. #TheGrownUpsVersionOfPlayingWithYourFood Makes ~1½ cups.

2 cups medium-packed fresh basil leaves
¾ teaspoon sea salt
2 medium cloves garlic
1½-2 tablespoons *Vegan Parmesan* (in Basics)
1 tablespoon fresh lemon juice
1 cup rinsed and drained cannellini beans
¼ cup raw pine nuts

Process all ingredients in a food processor and blend to form a paste. Taste and adjust seasonings. Add 2 tablespoons of water and process to incorporate. I think 2 tablespoons of water just about does it, but you can keep adding one tablespoon at a time to reach the consistency you like. Done!

Colorful Veggie-Basil Spread

A jar of grilled veggies is always a smart item to include in a well-stocked pantry. They can be used in all kinds of recipes, contributing fat (the oil), taste, and color. This spread freezes well, so consider stashing some for the holidays or an upcoming party. Schmear on crackers and toasted bagels.

Makes ~1 cup.

¾ cup jarred roasted red bell pepper
½ cup non-dairy butter spread, softened to room temperature
1 teaspoon-size fresh garlic
¼ cup packed basil leaves
¼ teaspoon salt
¼ teaspoon white pepper

Rinse bell pepper with warm water to remove excess oil and pat dry. Add to a food processor along with non-dairy butter, garlic, basil, salt and pepper. Process until smooth, scraping down the sides as needed. Taste and adjust seasoning.

Transfer to a ramekin or small bowl. Cover and refrigerate until ready to serve. Leave at room temperature ~10 minutes before serving.

Baked Pineapple with Basil and Peanuts

Adapted from chef Pichet Ong's recipe. If you've never baked pineapple before, this chewy treat might become a new favorite snack. I'm not usually a lover of pineapple on my pizza, but this is pretty fab on vegan mozzarella, and in particular, Daiya's Cheese Lover's Pizza. Sprinkle the cooked pineapple mixture on top during the last 10 minutes of baking.
#ItKindaLooksLikeHam
Makes 3½ cups.

2 ripe pineapples, peeled, cored and sliced into ¾"–1" rings
¼ cup demerara sugar
3 tablespoons fresh lime zest
3 tablespoons fresh basil, ground in a spice grinder
2 teaspoons Maldon sea salt
1 teaspoon freshly grated nutmeg
½ teaspoon chili powder
½ cup dry-roasted, unsalted peanuts

Preheat oven to 225°F. Line 2 large rimmed baking sheets with parchment paper and set aside.

Stack a few pineapple rings together and cut into 1" pieces. Divide between prepared baking sheets and place in a single layer. Bake, rotating pans and flipping pineapple after 2¼ hours. The chunks should be light golden brown, dried around the edges but still juicy in the center. Cook another 2¼ hours. Transfer pans to a cooling rack and cool to room temp, about 20 minutes.

In a large bowl, combine sugar, zest, basil, salt, nutmeg and chili powder. Stir well to mix, breaking up some of the larger salt flakes. Add pineapple and stir to coat. Add peanuts and stir to incorporate. Transfer to a serving bowl and serve. Store in a sealed container in the refrigerator.

Gluten-Free Zucchini-Basil Muffins

Ribbons of grated zucchini add visual interest, as does the savory and flavorful blend of basil, pine nuts and garlic. If gluten isn't an issue, use spelt or all-purpose flour. Consider these for breakfast or brunch, cut in half and topped with tofu scramble.
Makes 12 muffins.

2 tablespoons flax meal
2½ cups *Gluten-Free Flour Mix* (in Basics)
1 teaspoon baking soda
½ teaspoon baking powder
¾ teaspoon salt
1/3 cup nutritional yeast
2/3 cup non-dairy milk
¼ cup plus 3 tablespoons extra-virgin olive oil or *No-Oil Oil* (in Basics)
2 teaspoons freshly minced garlic
1½ cups shredded zucchini
½ cup packed fresh basil leaves, minced
½ cup pine nuts

In a small bowl, combine flax meal with 5 tablespoons water. Mix well and set aside.

Preheat oven to 425°F. Lightly grease a 12-cup muffin pan with a nonstick cooking spray and set aside.

In medium mixing bowl, sift gluten-free flour mix, baking soda, baking powder and salt. Stir in nutritional yeast and set aside.

In a large mixing bowl, whisk together non-dairy milk, oil and flax meal mixture until well blended. Fold in garlic.

Add dry ingredients to wet mixture and fold gently until just incorporated, being careful not to over-mix. Stir in zucchini, basil and pine nuts. Divide batter between muffin cups. Bake on the middle rack for 8 minutes, then lower heat to 350°F and cook 16-18 more minutes, or until a toothpick inserted into the center comes out clean. Cool on a wire rack 5 minutes before removing from pan. Serve warm.

Dreamy Basil Dressing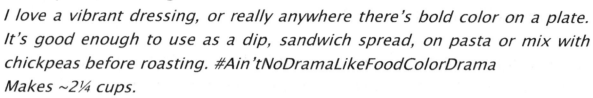

I love a vibrant dressing, or really anywhere there's bold color on a plate. It's good enough to use as a dip, sandwich spread, on pasta or mix with chickpeas before roasting. #Ain'tNoDramaLikeFoodColorDrama
Makes ~2¼ cups.

¼ cup raw sunflower seeds
1 cup unsweetened non-dairy milk
¾ cup silken tofu
1 tablespoon chia seeds
1 large stalk celery
2 tablespoons fresh lemon juice
Zest of a small lemon
1½ teaspoons freshly garlic
½ teaspoon onion powder
¼ teaspoon white pepper
¾ teaspoon salt
1 cup packed fresh basil

Place all ingredients in a high-speed blender and process on high until all basil flecks are gone. Taste and adjust seasoning.

Basil–Infused Honey

Use this flavorful honey on waffles, pancakes or French toast. Spoon a tablespoon onto non–dairy vanilla yogurt, fresh fruit slices, or stir into a cup of hot tea. You 're getting the idea. #Baklava,Anyone?
Makes 1 cup.

1 cup honey or Bee Free Honee®
½ teaspoon ground cinnamon
1 tablespoon brandy
4 large leaves from an upper stem of basil

Combine honey, cinnamon and brandy in a saucepan and heat over low heat.

Place basil in a sterilized jar and pour the warmed honey on top, covering the basil. Seal tightly and age for one week. Use a small fork to strain off the basil and discard. Store in the refrigerator in a tightly sealed container and use within 3 months.

Fennel, Tomato and Basil Casserole

This is an exceptional combination of flavors, and a little textural interest from the breadcrumbs. I could eat this all day long.
Makes 6 servings.

2 leeks, white parts only, cleaned well and thinly sliced
2 small fennel bulbs, trimmed and thinly sliced
2 teaspoons freshly minced garlic
2 cups rough chopped artichoke hearts
½ cup vegetable stock
¼ cup store-bought or homemade pesto
4 large ripe tomatoes, skins remove and thinly sliced
2 tablespoons minced black olives
1 cup fresh breadcrumbs
¼ cup chopped pine nuts
1 tablespoon extra-virgin olive

Preheat oven to 375°F.

Cover the bottom of a large skillet with 1/4" of water and bring to a boil. Lower heat to medium and add leeks, fennel and garlic. Cover and cook about 5 minutes, or until softened, checking mid-way and adding more water to keep from drying out. Remove from heat, add artichoke hearts and set aside.

In a small bowl, use a fork to combine stock and pesto until blended. Set aside.

Grease a 2-quart gratin baking dish lightly with non-stick cooking spray. Place fennel mixture on bottom and top with tomato slices. Season with a little salt and pepper to taste. Pour pesto–stock mixture over tomatoes and sprinkle with minced olives. Set aside.

In a small bowl, combine breadcrumbs, pine nuts and oil. Blend gently with a fork and sprinkle on top of gratin. Bake 40 minutes, or until tomatoes are tender and the top is browned. Let rest 5 minutes before serving.

Basil Focaccia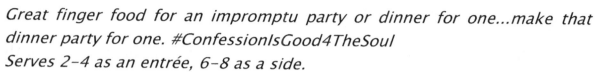

Great finger food for an impromptu party or dinner for one...make that dinner party for one. #ConfessionIsGood4TheSoul
Serves 2–4 as an entrée, 6–8 as a side.

2 cups loosely packed fresh basil leaves, plus more to garnish
2 medium garlic cloves, peeled
1/3 cup unsalted dry-roasted peanuts, plus 2 tablespoons to garnish
1–2 small fresh hot red chilies, stemmed and seeded
1 small avocado
½ teaspoon salt
3 tablespoons peanut oil
One 12" whole-wheat pizza dough

Preheat oven to 400°F.

In a food processor, combine basil, garlic, peanuts, chilies, avocado and salt. Process until a paste forms. With the machine running, add peanut oil through the feed tube and process until well incorporated. Taste and adjust seasoning. Set aside.

Punch pizza dough down. Lightly grease a 12-inch pizza pan or 9-by-13-inch baking sheet with non-stick cooking spray.

On a lightly floured work surface, roll out dough to fit your pan. Transfer to prepared pan and top with basil mixture, pressing lightly into the dough. Bake on the bottom rack 25–30 minutes, or until crust is golden brown. Top with additional basil and reserved chopped peanuts. Serve warm.

White Bean, Basil and Tomato Salad

Juicy, fresh tomatoes and basil straight from the garden perk up white beans, giving this combo lots of visual appeal. #RedWhite&Green
Makes 4-6 servings.

Salad

2 cups canned white beans, rinsed and well drained
Sea salt and freshly ground black pepper
1 cup gently packed fresh basil leaves, stems removed
7 medium, ripe tomatoes, ~2½ pounds

Vinaigrette

2 tablespoons fresh orange juice
1 tablespoon fresh lemon juice
1 tablespoon fresh lime juice
1/8 teaspoon sea salt
¼ cup olive oil or *No-Oil Oil* (in Basics)
¼ cup hot water

Place beans in a mixing bowl. Tear basil leaves into bite-size pieces and add to beans. Core tomatoes, cut into sixths, and then cut each sixth into thirds width-wise. Add to beans and season with salt and black pepper.

In a small mixing bowl, combine orange, lemon and lime juices and whisk with a fork. Add salt and whisk in oil and water. Taste for balance and adjust seasoning.

Pour half the vinaigrette into beans and stir to mix well. Taste and adjust seasoning, adding more vinaigrette as desired. Serve immediately or refrigerate 20 minutes to allow flavors to meld.

Green Beans with Basil

Because the ingredients are pretty basic and the method is simple, you might not expect this to be so full of flavor. That's the power of the herb. I've eaten the whole thing in one sitting. Double the recipe if you want to share, or have leftovers.

Makes a generous 2 cups, 2-4 servings.

12 ounces fresh green beans
½ cup diced red bell pepper, ~½ bell pepper
1 clove garlic, minced
1 thin scallion, green and white parts, minced
1/3 cup boiling water
3 tablespoons fresh basil, minced
1 tablespoon fresh lemon zest, ~1 lemon
½ teaspoon salt
1 tablespoon lemon juice
Freshly ground black pepper, to taste

Wash and trim bean ends, de-string and set aside.

Cover the bottom of a large frying pan with ¼" water and set heat to medium. Add red pepper and cook 3 minutes, adding more water if needed to keep the pan from completely drying out. Add garlic and scallions and cook 1 minute, stirring until softened. Add green beans, boiling water, basil, zest and salt. Cover and simmer 5 minutes, until tender but still crisp.

Remove from heat and stir in lemon juice and freshly ground pepper. Taste and adjust seasoning. Serve warm.

Split Pea Soup with Basil

Cut the cooking time down by soaking the peas overnight, saving yourself at least a good hour. That's more than enough time to make a batch of Baconut to have for garnishing.

Makes 8 servings.

1¾ cups split peas, soaked overnight
1½ cups rough chopped yellow onion
3 cloves garlic, smashed (not minced)
4 quarts plus 1 cup vegetable stock
3 cups diced potato (skins on and scrubbed clean)
3/4 cup packed basil leaves plus small leaves to garnish
1 tablespoon sea salt
1 tablespoon black pepper
½ cup *Baconut,* optional, to garnish (in Basics)

Add 3 tablespoons water to a large stockpot along with the onion and garlic and bring to a boil. Lower heat to medium and cook 5 minutes, stirring frequently. Add more water if the pan starts to dry out, but if it's near the 5 minute mark, no need to add more.

Rinse peas in a strainer and add to stockpot, along with stock and potato. Bring to a boil, lower heat to a simmer. Add basil, salt and pepper. Cover and cook 40 minutes, until peas have softened.

Cool slightly, then purée in batches in a high-speed blender. Return to saucepan, taste and adjust seasoning. Reheat before serving. Garnish each serving with basil and a generous pinch of *Baconut.*

Green Velvet Basil Soup

This soup is rich and satisfying, not to mention a beautiful color. A "complete meal" soup, you might as well toast up some French bread, pour yourself a glass of wine or two, and binge-watch Love Your Garden.
#ItDoesn'tHave2BComplicated
Makes 4-6 servings.

1 medium onion, diced
3 garlic cloves, minced
1 pound fresh spinach, freshly washed, no need to pat dry
1 cup packed fresh basil leaves
3 cups vegetable stock
1½ cups non-dairy milk
½ teaspoon sea salt
Freshly ground black pepper
Dash cayenne pepper
Dash of freshly grated nutmeg
4 tablespoons *Vegan Parmesan* (in Basics)
6 small basil leaf clusters, to garnish

Cover the bottom of a stockpot with 1/8" of water. Bring to a boil, lower heat and add onion, cooking to soften. Add garlic and cook 1 minute.

Add spinach to stockpot and lower heat to a simmer. Cook for 4 minutes, until spinach has wilted. Add basil and stock and bring to medium heat for 5 minutes. Add non-dairy milk, salt, pepper, cayenne and nutmeg. Stir well to incorporate. Taste and adjust seasoning.

In a high-speed blender, purée soup in batches. Return to stockpot and stir in 3 tablespoons vegan parmesan. Warm soup over low heat for 2–3 minutes, stirring occasionally. Ladle into warm bowls and garnish with remaining vegan parmesan and basil leaves.

Potato and Pesto Pizza

Lightly adapted from Carolyn Dille and Susan Belsinger's Herbs In the Kitchen. This is a surprisingly delicious combination. #CrowdPleaser
Makes two 9-inch pizzas. I'm not gonna tell you how many people that serves. #NoJudgmentHere

Two packages of 13-ounce pre-made pizza dough, cornmeal or whole wheat
12 whole new potatoes, about 2" in diameter, assorted colors are good
1 red onion
¼ cup olive oil plus 1½ tablespoons
5-6 garlic cloves, 2 unpeeled and mashed, the others peeled
1 cup packed basil leaves
½ cup *Vegan Parmesan* (in Basics)
Salt and pepper to taste

Preheat oven to 350°F.

Scrub potatoes, dry and rub with the 1½ tablespoons olive oil. Cut onion in half length-wise, then into 1/8" slices. Place potatoes and onions in a baking dish with the 2 unpeeled, mashed garlic cloves. Cover and place in oven 35-40 minutes, until tender. Remove from oven and discard the smashed garlic. Transfer potatoes to a cutting board and cool to room temperature.

Add peeled garlic and basil to a food processor and blend into a smooth paste. Add vegan parmesan and remaining ¼ cup olive oil. Taste and adjust seasoning. If desired, add a little water to thin.

Slice potatoes into 1/4" thick pieces and set aside.

Heat oven to 450°F. Position one of the racks to the lowest shelf.

Lightly grease a pizza pan or baking sheet with non-stick spray. Form each package of dough into 9-inch rounds or whatever shape fits your pan. Lightly brush with additional olive oil. Divide potato and onion slices between dough and season lightly with salt and pepper.

Place pan on the lowest oven rack. Bake 5-6 minutes or until crusts are puffed around the edges and light golden brown. Remove from oven and divide pesto between pizzas, spreading over potatoes and onions.

Return to oven for 6-8 minutes, or until bottom crust is done and pesto gets bubbly. Remove from oven and transfer to a cutting board for 10 minutes to cool. Slice and serve warm.

Spicy Basil Mayo

Use this bright green mayo on grilled tomatoes, sandwich wraps and potato or pasta salad.
Makes ~1¼ cup.

1 garlic clove
6 ounces soft silken tofu
2 teaspoons fresh lemon juice or apple cider vinegar
2 teaspoons Dijon mustard
¼ teaspoon sea salt
½ cup basil
¼ cup grapeseed oil or *No-Oil Oil* (in Basics)

Add garlic, tofu, lemon juice, Dijon, salt and basil to a high-speed blender and process until smooth.

While pulsing, slowly add the oil. Blend until emulsified. Taste and adjust seasoning, adding more salt or lemon juice.

Basil-Infused Orange Granita

Move your dessert game up a notch by serving this inside frozen, hollowed-out orange shells. #LittleOrbsOfGoodness
Makes 2 cups; 2-4 servings.

½ cup plus 2 tablespoons sugar
2 cups water
1¼ cups freshly squeezed orange juice
¼ cup freshly squeezed lemon juice
½ cup packed fresh basil leaves
¼ cup Orange Curaçao, Triple Sec or Cointreau
4 top clusters of small basil leaves, to garnish

In a medium saucepan, add sugar and water and bring to medium heat. Stir until sugar dissolves. Remove from heat and stir in orange and lemon juices, basil and Curaçao. When cooled, cover and refrigerate overnight to infuse.

Use a fine-mesh strainer to strain out basil, pressing with the back of a wooden spoon to extract as much flavor as possible. Discard basil. Pour mixture into ice cube trays, cover and freeze until firm. When ready to serve, process cubes in a high-speed blender. Garnish each serving with basil clusters.

Wild Rice, Quinoa and Basil Pilaf

A couple of surprising ingredients contribute to this colorful and flavorsome pilaf. This is a good pot-luck dish, even when made a day in advance. Wild rice has a nutty flavor and provides another textural element. #It'sNotAlwaysAboutColor
Makes 8-10 servings.

One 2.75-ounce box instant wild rice
2 cups veggie stock
1 cup quinoa, rinsed in a fine-mesh strainer
½ teaspoon sea salt
1½ tablespoons organic, cold-pressed, unrefined coconut oil
1 cup diced carrot
1 cup diced celery
1 cup diced yellow onion
½ cup diced shallots
1 cup roasted and peeled chestnuts, rough chopped
½ cup golden raisins
½ cup gently packed fresh basil, minced
¼ teaspoon black pepper
½ cup raw whole cashews or large pieces

Prepare wild rice according to directions.

In a medium sauce pan, bring stock, quinoa and salt to a boil. Cover, lower heat to a simmer and cook 15 minutes. Remove from heat and keep covered 5 minutes. Fluff with a fork.

Add wild rice and quinoa to a casserole dish and stir well to mix. Set aside.

Bring a large frying pan to medium-high heat. Add oil to coat the bottom. Add carrots, celery, onions and shallots. Lower heat to medium and cook, stirring regularly, for 12 minutes, or until soft. Add chestnuts, raisins, basil and pepper and stir to incorporate. Cover and cook 3 minutes or until warmed throughout.

Bring a small, dry frying pan to medium-low heat. Add cashews and toast, stirring regularly, until browned. Remove from pan and set aside to cool.

Add carrot mixture to wild rice and quinoa and stir well. Taste and adjust seasoning.

Rough-chop cashews when cool enough to handle and fold into pilaf. Serve warm.

Succotash with Basil

Eat by itself or use it as a chunky salad dressing over of a bed of mixed salad greens. For a quick supper dish, serve warm over rice noodles, farro, or brown rice. #Options
Makes 4-6 servings.

½ large red onion, diced
½ red bell pepper, seeded and cut small dice
½ green bell pepper, seeded and cut small dice
½ orange bell pepper, seeded and cut small dice
Kernels from 3 fresh ears sweet corn, uncooked
¾ cup canned lima beans
1 jalapeño, seeded and diced
½ can kidney beans, rinsed well
1½ teaspoons salt, divided
4 tomatillos, husks and stems removed
2 pickling or Kirby cucumbers, sliced and quartered
½ cup packed fresh basil, minced
Chili powder, to garnish

Add ¼" water to the bottom of a frying pan and bring to a boil. Lower heat to medium and add onion and peppers. Cook 2-3 minutes, stirring constantly to soften. Add more water to keep pan from drying out.

Stir in corn, lima beans, jalapeño, kidney beans and 1 teaspoon salt. Cover and cook 3-5 minutes, stirring occasionally. Add a little water if needed to keep the pan from completely drying out.

In a blender or food processor, combine tomatillos and remaining ½ teaspoon salt. Process until smooth. Add to pan with corn and stir to incorporate. Cook 2 minutes.

Add cucumber and cook another minute to heat throughout. Stir in basil. Taste and adjust seasoning. Transfer to a serving dish and sprinkle lightly with chili powder. Serve warm.

Silky Basil Applesauce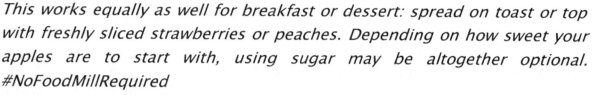

This works equally as well for breakfast or dessert: spread on toast or top with freshly sliced strawberries or peaches. Depending on how sweet your apples are to start with, using sugar may be altogether optional. #NoFoodMillRequired

Makes 5½ cups, or 6–8 servings.

6 cooking apples, (McIntosh, Braeburn or Gala), skins intact, scrubbed
  clean
3 cups apple cider or apple juice
1 cup packed large whole basil leaves, divided
4 whole cloves
One 3" cinnamon stick
2 tablespoons fresh lemon juice
½ teaspoon fresh lemon zest
¼ cup turbinado or demerara sugar, if needed (use brown sugar for tart
  apples)

Core and rough chop apples into uniform 1½ –2" pieces. Add to a 2-quart stockpot along with cider, ½ cup basil, cloves and cinnamon stick. Bring to medium heat, cover and cook 25–30 minutes, stirring occasionally, until apples are soft but not over-cooked.

Remove cloves and cinnamon and discard. Taste a piece of apple, and if the basil flavor isn't as strong as you'd like, keep a little in the pot to blend up with the apples; discard the rest. Stir in lemon juice and zest. Use a spider strainer to transfer apples and half the cooking liquid to a high-speed blender. Purée.

Add more liquid from the pot as desired, keeping in mind that the applesauce will thicken as it cools. Keep sauce in the blender and cool to room temperature.

Taste for sweetness and if needed, add 1 tablespoon sugar at a time and process to incorporate.

Transfer to a sealable container and store in the refrigerator. Top each serving with reserved basil, julienned.

Basil–Orange Butter

Flavored butters are just too easy to make. For a special occasion, use molds or cookie cutters to create fun shapes and dress up your table. Makes ½ cup.

½ cup non-dairy butter, at room temperature
1 tablespoon freshly minced basil
½ tablespoon freshly minced chives
Zest of one orange
1/8 teaspoon sea salt
1/8 teaspoon white pepper

Place all ingredients in a small bowl. Use a fork to mix everything together well. Taste and adjust seasoning. Refrigerate and use within 2 weeks.

Roasted Shishito Peppers with Basil Dipping Sauce

In my book, finger foods are some of the best foods on the planet. These quick-roasting little morsels are seriously fun to nosh on. #HardToQuit Makes 4-5 servings or 2 really hungry people. #TrueStory

18 ounces fresh whole shishito peppers, rinsed and patted dry
1 tablespoon organic, cold-pressed, unrefined coconut oil, melted
A generous pinch sea salt

Dipping Sauce
1/3 cup packed fresh basil
1/3 cup plain non-dairy yogurt
1 tablespoon extra-virgin olive oil
1 tablespoon fresh lemon juice
1½ teaspoon minced fresh garlic
¾ teaspoon cumin
¼ teaspoon sea salt
A few grinds of fresh black pepper

Preheat oven to 450°F.

Place peppers in a large mixing bowl and drizzle with oil. Stir to coat well and place in a single layer on a rimmed baking sheet. Sprinkle with salt and place in oven. Roast 5-7 minutes, until charred on one side. Turn over and roast another 5 minutes. Remove from oven and transfer to a serving plate. Serve warm with dipping sauce.

To make sauce, place all ingredients in a mini-food processor or small container for a stick blender and process until smooth. Taste and adjust seasoning. Transfer to a small bowl and serve in the middle of the peppers.

Cantaloupe with Basil-Infused Wine

After marinating in red wine, cantaloupe takes on some of the colors of a sunset. Inhale deeply, exhale slowly and think of your last vacation.
#VacationMemories
Makes 4 servings.

2 cups light red wine, (Beaujolais, Gamay or Pinot Noir)
4 tablespoons sugar
One ripe 3-pound cantaloupe, halved and seeds removed
2 tablespoons packed basil leaves, chopped
1 small lemon
4 small top basil clusters, to garnish

In a small saucepan, add wine and bring to low heat. Wine should be steaming but not simmering.

Add sugar and stir to dissolve completely. Remove from heat and pour into a medium ceramic or glass bowl. Stir in basil and cover. Set aside to infuse and cool completely.

When completely cooled, use a fine-mesh strainer to strain out the basil, pressing with the back of a wooden spoon to extract as much flavor as possible. Discard basil.

Use a small-sized melon baller to scoop cantaloupe. Add balls to wine infusion. You should have ~4 cups fruit.

Peel lemon and cut the peel into sixths. Set aside the lemon for another use. Add peel to cantaloupe and wine. Cover and refrigerate 30 minutes.

Remove lemon strips and before serving and discard. Divide melon balls along with a little of the liquid between 4 stemmed glasses. Garnish with basil and serve.

Eggplant Spread with Basil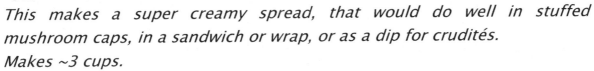

This makes a super creamy spread, that would do well in stuffed mushroom caps, in a sandwich or wrap, or as a dip for crudités.
Makes ~3 cups.

2 medium eggplant, peeled and sliced ½" thick
1 yellow onion, chopped
4 garlic cloves, minced
1 jalapeño
¾ cup packed fresh basil leaves
½ teaspoon liquid smoke
1 teaspoon lemon juice
¾ cup raw walnuts, rough chopped
½ teaspoon sea salt
Freshly ground black pepper

Salt both sides of eggplant slices and set on a dish cloth for 30 minutes to drain. Pat dry and cut into 1" cubes.

Add enough water to a frying pan to thinly coat the bottom 1/8"-¼". Bring to medium heat and add onion, garlic and jalapeño. Cook 5-7 minutes, until softened, adding more water if necessary to keep anything from sticking. Add eggplant and cook 10-15 minutes, stirring regularly, until it starts to brown. Add basil and cook 1-2 minutes until softened. Lower heat to the lowest setting and add liquid smoke. Cover and steam 10 minutes, until tender.

Transfer mixture to a high-speed blender and process until smooth. Add lemon juice, walnuts, salt and black pepper and blend until smooth. Taste and adjust seasonings. Transfer to a serving bowl and serve.

Pomegranate-Basil-Lime Salad Dressing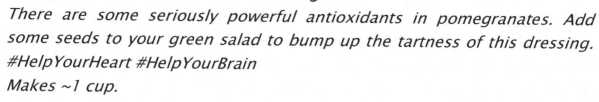

There are some seriously powerful antioxidants in pomegranates. Add some seeds to your green salad to bump up the tartness of this dressing. #HelpYourHeart #HelpYourBrain

Makes ~1 cup.

½ cup unsweetened pomegranate juice
¼ cup extra-virgin olive oil or *No-Oil Oil* (in Basics)
Zest of 1 lime
½ cup loosely packed fresh basil
2 tablespoons lime juice
1 tablespoon coconut sugar
1/8 teaspoon sea salt
½ cup fresh pomegranate seeds, to garnish, optional

Use a stick blender and a tall, narrow container to blend juice, oil, zest, basil, lime juice, sugar and salt until smooth. Taste and adjust seasoning. Transfer to a Mason jar and refrigerate before use. Shake well before serving.

Watermelon Salad with Watermelon–Basil Vinaigrette

This vinaigrette pairs two standouts from any summer garden-- watermelon and basil. That duo can spark a lot of new dishes; it's got me thinking about a mojito...#WatermelonInspo
Salad serves 4 as an entrée; ~4 cups dressing.

Dressing
4 cups seedless watermelon, chopped, with juices
¼ cup red onion, rough chopped
1 medium celery stalk, chopped
2 tablespoons agave
¼ cup champagne vinegar
1 tablespoon chia seeds
¼ cup packed fresh basil leaves
¾ teaspoon sea salt
¼ teaspoon black pepper

Salad
One whole, round slice watermelon, quartered, to serve
12 ounces assorted fresh baby field greens
2 tablespoons raw almonds, rough chopped
2 tablespoons raw pumpkin seeds

In a high-speed blender, combine watermelon, onion, celery, agave, vinegar, chia, basil, salt and black pepper. Process until there are no visible basil flecks. Taste and adjust seasoning. If the watermelon wasn't very juicy, you may need to add a little water to cut the vinegar. Start with 1/8 cup, if needed.

Refrigerate at least 15 minutes before serving to allow chia seeds to thicken the dressing. Foam may form on top, so shake or stir well before serving.

Cut each watermelon quarter into 3 wedges. Place salad greens on a platter, top with watermelon triangles, and sprinkle with nuts and seeds. Serve with vinaigrette. If you've got a grill going, throw the watermelon quarters on to get some nice grill marks.

Stuffed Zucchini with Lentils, Veggies and Basil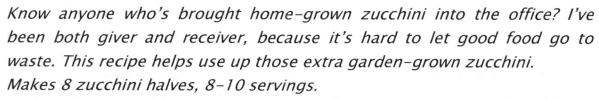

Know anyone who's brought home-grown zucchini into the office? I've been both giver and receiver, because it's hard to let good food go to waste. This recipe helps use up those extra garden-grown zucchini.
Makes 8 zucchini halves, 8-10 servings.

4 medium-large zucchini, washed and stems trimmed (10" in length)
½ cup raw cashews
1 cup diced yellow onion
1 tablespoon freshly minced garlic
1 cup diced celery
1 cup diced carrot
2 cups cooked lentils
1 cup cooked quinoa
½ cup cooked oatmeal
¼ cup packed fresh basil, minced
2 tablespoons fresh parsley, minced
1 teaspoon Bragg's Organic Sprinkle Seasoning
1 teaspoon cumin
¼ teaspoon sea salt
Freshly ground black pepper
¼-½ cup tomato juice, optional, if mixture is too dry

Cut zucchini in half lengthwise and scoop out seeds, leaving a ½" border. Set aside.

Preheat oven to 375°F. Lightly grease two 8-by-12-inch baking pans with non-stick spray and set aside.

Place cashews in a food processor and grind to a coarse meal. Set aside.

Add 4–5 tablespoons water to the bottom of a large frying pan. Add onion, garlic, celery and carrots and bring to medium–high heat. Cook 7–8 minutes until soft, adding more water to keep from drying out completely. Transfer to a large mixing bowl and add cashew meal, lentils, quinoa and oatmeal and mix well. Add, basil, parsley, Bragg's seasoning, cumin, salt and pepper and mix until well incorporated. If mixture is too runny, add more ground nuts, quinoa, lentils or oatmeal. If it's too dry, add one tablespoon tomato juice at a time until you have a soft, moist mixture that holds together. When you spoon it around the bowl, it should readily stick to wherever you've moved it.

Spoon mixture into prepared zucchini halves and press into a nice smooth mound. Bake 45 minutes, or until zucchini is tender. Cool 10 minutes before slicing and serve warm.

Choke-Mushroom-Basil Mash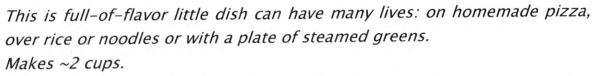

*This is full-of-flavor little dish can have many lives: on homemade pizza,
over rice or noodles or with a plate of steamed greens.*
Makes ~2 cups.

One 15-ounce can hearts of palm or artichoke hearts, water-packed
½ cup button mushrooms, rough chopped
1/8 cup minced red onion
½ teaspoon Dijon mustard
1 tablespoon lemon juice
1 tablespoon extra-virgin olive oil or *No-Oil Oil* (in Basics)
1 tablespoon warm water
1 clove garlic, minced
1/8 cup packed fresh basil, chiffonade
Salt and black pepper, to taste

Drain, rinse and quarter hearts of palm or artichoke hearts. Transfer to a
large mixing bowl and add mushrooms. Use a stick blender to mash,
keeping some small chunks. Stir in red onion and set aside.

In a small bowl, combine Dijon and lemon juice. Slowly whisk in oil and
warm water. Fold in garlic and basil. Add a pinch salt and pepper and taste
for balance, adjusting seasoning. Pour over hearts of palm or artichoke
hearts and stir to incorporate. Serve at room temperature.

Asparagus-Corn Salad with Basil

I look forward to sweet corn in the summer. Whether I grow it or pick some up from the farmer's market, I love eating it raw. Here, it's combined with basil, tomatoes, and asparagus for an almost raw dish. Serve on top of some fresh salad greens as a colorful, chunky "salad dressing."
#SneakingInMoreVegetables
Makes 4 servings.

1 pound asparagus, washed and tough ends removed
3 ears fresh ripe corn
1 cup cherry tomatoes
2 tablespoons freshly minced red onion
1 tablespoon fresh lemon juice
¼ cup packed fresh basil, chiffonade
Salt and freshly ground black pepper

Bring a large stockpot filled halfway with salted water to a boil. Add asparagus and cook 3 minutes. Remove with a spider strainer and submerge into an ice bath. When cooled to the touch, remove from water and shake off excess. Slice into 1½" lengths and place in a large bowl. Set aside.

Use a sharp knife to cut the corn from the cobs and add to asparagus. Quarter tomatoes and add to asparagus. Set aside.

In a small bowl, combine onion, lemon juice, basil and a pinch salt and pepper. Pour over asparagus mixture and toss well. Taste and adjust seasoning. Serve at room temperature or refrigerate 20 minutes before serving.

Basil Lemonade

Vary the recipe by using freshly squeezed orange juice or canned pear nectar in place of the lemon juice. #TheManyFriendsOfBasil
Makes 4½ cups, 4–6 servings.

½ cup packed fresh basil
4 tablespoons sugar
4 cups water
½ cup plus 2 tablespoons lemon juice
Fresh small basil leaves, to garnish

In a 2-quart glass bowl, combine basil and sugar. Using a wooden spoon, mash leaves into the sugar until thoroughly bruised. Add water and lemon juice. Stir until sugar is dissolved, 1–2 minutes. Taste and add more sugar if desired.

Strain out basil by pouring mixture through a fine-mesh strainer into ice-filled glasses. Garnish with small basil leaves and serve.

Raw Chocolate and Basil Truffles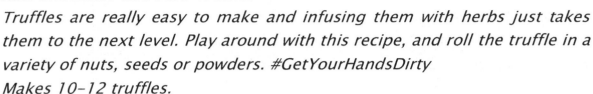

Truffles are really easy to make and infusing them with herbs just takes them to the next level. Play around with this recipe, and roll the truffle in a variety of nuts, seeds or powders. #GetYourHandsDirty
Makes 10-12 truffles.

2 cups Medjool dates, pitted and softened in hot water, well drained
½ cup semi-sweet chocolate chips, melted
¼ cup finely ground almonds
¼ cup packed fresh basil
2 tablespoons organic, cold-pressed, unrefined coconut oil, divided
3 tablespoons coconut flour
2 tablespoons unsweetened cocoa powder, plus ¼ cup for rolling
½ teaspoon sea salt
Fresh small fresh basil leaves to garnish

In a food processor, combine dates, chocolate, almonds, basil, 1¾ tablespoons coconut oil, 2 tablespoons cocoa powder and salt. Process to form a paste, scraping down sides as necessary. If mixture is too moist, add more coconut flour, ½ tablespoon at a time.

Place remaining ¼ cup cocoa powder in a small bowl and set aside.

Coat your hands with remaining ¼ tablespoon coconut oil. Form mixture into ¾" balls, then place in the bowl of cocoa powder, and roll to cover completely. Press small basil leaves in the tops and refrigerate half an hour before serving.

Basil-Mushroom Chili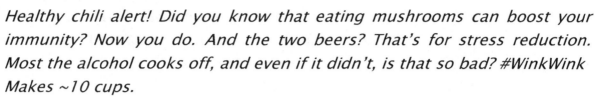

Healthy chili alert! Did you know that eating mushrooms can boost your immunity? Now you do. And the two beers? That's for stress reduction. Most the alcohol cooks off, and even if it didn't, is that so bad? #WinkWink Makes ~10 cups.

1 tablespoon organic, cold-pressed, unrefined coconut oil
1 pound fresh cremini mushrooms, stems cleaned, trimmed, chopped
Two 12-ounce bottles dark beer, divided
1 tablespoon freshly minced garlic
¼ cup freshly minced shallots
1 fresh jalapeño, minced
3 tablespoons chili powder
1 tablespoon cumin
Two 15-ounce cans crushed tomatoes
One 15-ounce can dark red kidney beans, rinsed and well drained
1/3 cup maple sugar
1½ teaspoons sea salt
½ teaspoon black pepper
Four fresh 6" corn tortillas, ripped into small pieces
½ cup freshly minced basil
2 tablespoons freshly minced parsley

Bring a large stockpot to medium heat. Add coconut oil and spread to coat the bottom. Add mushrooms and one beer bottle and lower heat to medium-low. Cook 8-10 minutes, stirring occasionally. As mushrooms soften, use a spatula to break up any large pieces.

Add garlic, shallots, jalapeño, chili powder and cumin and stir well to incorporate. Cook 3-4 minutes. Add remaining beer, tomatoes, beans, sugar, salt, pepper, tortilla pieces, basil and parsley. Bring to a boil, lower heat to medium-low and cook 25-30 minutes. Taste and adjust seasoning. Serve warm.

Blueberry–Basil Vinegar

This is a beautiful infused vinegar, and shows especially well in a frosted or clear glass bottle. Use instead of white vinegar in recipes, or splash on fresh cut stone fruit before serving. Double the recipe if you want to gift a jar. #I'mEasilyExcitedByColor
Makes ~1 cup.

A dozen large basil leaves, about 5" in length each, rinsed and dried completely
1 cup fresh blueberries, rinsed and patted dried
1 cup white or champagne vinegar
6 whole black peppercorns

Bruise basil and blueberries with a wooden spoon. Place in a sterilized Mason jar along with peppercorns and cover with vinegar. Seal and shake well.

Place in a cool, dark place for 1 week, and shake daily. Use a fine-mesh strainer to strain out the solids and discard. Transfer to a sterilized Mason jar, seal tightly and label. Store in refrigerator and use within 2 months.

Roasted Spiced Pecans with Basil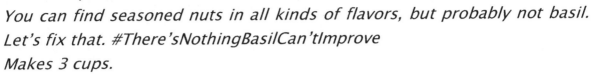

You can find seasoned nuts in all kinds of flavors, but probably not basil.
Let's fix that. #There'sNothingBasilCan'tImprove
Makes 3 cups.

3 cups raw pecan halves
2 tablespoons organic, cold-pressed, unrefined coconut oil, melted
2 tablespoons packed fresh basil, ground in a spice grinder
1 teaspoon vanilla extract
1 teaspoon cinnamon
Pinch sea salt

Preheat oven to 350°F.

Spread nuts on a dry, rimmed baking sheet and bake, stirring occasionally, 10-12 minutes.

In a small bowl, combine melted coconut oil, basil, extract, cinnamon and salt. Remove nuts from oven and pour oil mixture on top. Stir to evenly distribute seasoning. Return to oven and bake 5-6 minutes, stirring midway. Remove from oven and transfer to another cookie sheet to cool. Store refrigerated in sealed container. Nuts will keep – well, really, will they??

CORIANDRUM SATIVUM: CILANTRO

Growing Tips

Cilantro, also known as Chinese parsley, is an annual herb that's easy to grow provided it gets good sun.

Cilantro has a short growing cycle, so if you have space, plant another one in the ground every three weeks to keep you in steady supply.

A perk of having cilantro planted in your garden is that butterflies love it. Staggering planting as suggested above will insure these delicate visitors are regularly in your garden.

To preserve cilantro's desired flavor, keep it from bolting, otherwise, the taste becomes bitter. Try growing it earlier in the year. It's the heat of summer that makes it bolt.

The seeds of cilantro are known as coriander, a widely used spice with a very different flavor profile from cilantro. Coriander has a nutty, earthy, slightly citrusy flavor.

Collect seeds after the stalk has turned brown and dry. Place stalks in a paper bag head first, and tie it at the base. Hang to dry so the bag will catch the seeds as they dry.

Varieties

If you've grown cilantro before, you know well the common complaint that it bolts. Fortunately, there are some varieties that are slow bolting, and even bolt-resistant.

Calypso is slow to bolt variety and high-yielding. Win-Win.

Confetti is slow to bolt, high-yielding, mild-tasting with feathery leaves not typical of cilantro.

Culantro, aka *Spiny Coriander* is common in Latin and Central American cuisines. The flavor is stronger and sharper than cilantro. Be sure to remove the spines and cook culantro. You can substitute culantro for cilantro, just use less. Since you're wondering, yes, culantro is the correct spelling.

Jantar is a high-yield cilantro, and slow to bolt.

Leisure is a high-yielding cilantro with large leaves. It's known for not going to seed in warmer months.

Long Standing is another variety known for not going to seed in warmer months.

Pokey Joe is slow to bolt and mild tasting.

Santo is fast growing with dark green leaves.

Vietnamese Cilantro is known as *rau ram* and doesn't look like cilantro at all. It has long, pointed, dark leaves, sometimes with a dark stamp mark on them. It bolts less than regular cilantro.

Cooking Tips

If you're between plants and have to purchase cilantro by the bunch, one bunch store-bought equals 3 cups chopped.

Don't be tempted to substitute parsley for cilantro. All herbs have a unique contribution to a dish, and there's just no substitute for fresh cilantro.

In some Asian markets, you may find cilantro bunches sold with their roots intact.

Corn Pie with Tomatillo Cilantro Salsa

Marinated Black Beans with Jalapeno & Cilantro

@Gail_Herndon_Huskins

Quick Veggie Pickles with Cilantro

Cantaloupe & Rice Salad with Cilantro Dressing

Roasted Sweet Potatoes and Poblanos with Cilantro Garlic Sauce

Baked Apple Rings with Curry & Cilantro

Raw Beet & Rhubarb Slaw with Cilantro Dressing

Quick Watermelon-Cilantro Soup

Coconut Cilantro Lime Shortbread

Banana Lentil Soup with Cilantro

Pea and Asparagus Guacamole with Cilantro

Verde Claro Soup with Cilantro

Smokey Black-Eyed Pea Dip with Cilantro on Toast Points

No-Churn Cilantro Nice Cream

CILANTRO RECIPES

Substitute 1 teaspoon-dried cilantro for every tablespoon fresh

Cilantro pairs well with apple, asparagus, avocado, banana, beans, beets, cantaloupe, carrots, cashews, cauliflower, chocolate, corn, coconut, cucumber, curry, eggplant, garlic, ginger, green chiles, jalapeño, lentils, lime, mango, onion, orange, peas, quinoa, radish, rhubarb, rice, sweet potatoes, tomatillos, and watermelon.

Avocado, Mango and Cilantro Salsa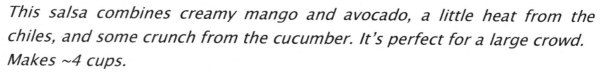

This salsa combines creamy mango and avocado, a little heat from the chiles, and some crunch from the cucumber. It's perfect for a large crowd. Makes ~4 cups.

1 ripe avocado, pitted and cut small dice
1 ripe mango, pitted and cut small dice
1 large, ripe tomato, seeded and cut small dice
1 cup Persian cucumber, ends removed, sliced and quartered
3 green onions, white and green parts, cut thinly on the diagonal
One 4-ounce can fire-roasted diced green chiles
4 tablespoons fresh lime juice
Zest of 1 lime
½ cup cilantro, minced
½ teaspoon cumin
½ teaspoon sea salt
¼ teaspoon red pepper flakes

Combine all ingredients in a medium bowl and mix well. Taste and adjust seasoning. Serve fresh.

Cantaloupe and Rice Salad with Cilantro Dressing
Lightly adapted from an old Los Angeles Times recipe.
#LooksLikeAPartyInABowl
Makes 6-8 servings.

1½ cups uncooked white rice
1¼ teaspoons salt, divided
¼ cup plus 1 tablespoon extra-virgin olive oil
¼ cup plus 1 tablespoon lime juice
1 teaspoon sugar
½ teaspoon cumin
¼ teaspoon black pepper
3 cups medium diced cantaloupe
1 cup gently packed fresh cilantro, rough chopped
1 cup diced celery
2/3 cup green onions, white and green parts thinly sliced on the diagonal
One 4-ounce can diced green chiles, well drained

In a medium stockpot, bring 2½ cups water to a boil. Add rice and the ¼ teaspoon salt. Reduce heat to low, cover and cook 20 minutes, until all water is absorbed. Remove from heat and keep covered. Let stand 5 minutes. Transfer to a large serving bowl and refrigerate uncovered.

In a small bowl mix oil, lime juice, sugar, cumin, black pepper and remaining 1 teaspoon salt. Whisk until smooth. Taste and adjust seasoning. Stir into chilled rice.

Add cantaloupe, cilantro, celery, onions and green chiles and toss to incorporate. Refrigerate 30 minutes before serving.

Green Apple and Cilantro Salad Dressing

Adapted from Jean-Marie Josselin's A Taste of Hawaii. Ginger juice really makes this recipe, and powdered ginger isn't a viable substitute. It's easy to make: after grating about one and a half to two times the amount of ginger juice needed, squeeze the pulp between your fingers, letting the juice fill a tablespoon. One and a half tablespoons grated ginger yields about 1 tablespoon juice. #ShhhhhhhhSecretIngredient
Makes 1½ cups.

½ large Granny Smith apple, cored and rough chopped
½ cup gently packed cilantro, leaves and stems
2 tablespoons fresh lime juice
¼ cup champagne vinegar
1½ tablespoons ginger juice
½ teaspoon tamari or soy sauce
¼ teaspoon freshly ground black pepper
1/3 cup extra-virgin olive oil or *No-Oil Oil* (in Basics)

Combine all ingredients in a high-speed blender and process until smooth. Serve immediately and store in a sealed container in the refrigerator. Dressing will keep for 5–7 days.

Green Chile–Orange–Cilantro Salad Dressing

Inspired by Mary McDougall's recipe, from one of their enlightening weekend programs in Santa Rosa, CA. For more about their programs and free recipes, visit DrMcDougall.com.
Makes 1¼ cups.

1 cup diced green chiles
1 cup fresh orange juice
½ cup cucumber, roughly chopped
¼ cup packed cilantro leaves and stems
½ teaspoon-size garlic clove
¼ teaspoon cumin
1/8 teaspoon black pepper

Combine all ingredients in a high-speed blender and process until smooth. Refrigerate until using.

Coconut-Cilantro-Lime Shortbread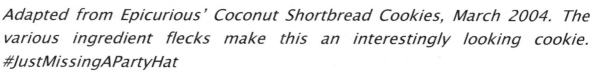

Adapted from Epicurious' Coconut Shortbread Cookies, March 2004. The various ingredient flecks make this an interestingly looking cookie. #JustMissingAPartyHat

Makes ~32 cookies.

½ cup unsweetened shredded coconut
2 cups all-purpose flour, sifted
¼ teaspoon baking powder
1/8 teaspoon salt
1 cup non-dairy butter, (2 sticks) at room temperature
¾ cup powdered sugar
4 teaspoons fresh lime zest
1 teaspoon vanilla extract
½ cup fresh cilantro, minced

Bring a small, dry frying pan to medium heat. Add coconut and stir constantly until lightly toasted, about a minute. Remove from heat and transfer to a plate to cool.

In a medium bowl, whisk together flour, baking powder and salt and set aside.

In a large mixing bowl, beat non-dairy butter, powdered sugar, zest and vanilla for 3 minutes. Fold in toasted coconut and cilantro. Stir in flour mixture ½ cup at a time.

Divide dough in half and roll into 7" long logs. Wrap in parchment or soy-derived wax paper and chill 3 hours.

Preheat oven to 350°F and line 2 baking sheets with parchment. Slice each log into sixteen ¼" thick cookies. Bake 7 minutes, then rotate baking sheets. Bake 8 more minutes, and edges turn lightly golden. Cool 5 minutes before transferring to a wire rack.

Quick Veggie Pickles with Cilantro

Hot pink, leaf green and white. I love these colors together and the pickled little bite these give to sandwiches, wraps and salads. To make ginger juice, use a microplane to grate one and a half to two times the amount of desired juice, then squeeze the pulp with your fingers into a measuring spoon. One and a half teaspoons grated ginger yields about 1 teaspoon juice.

Makes 3 cups.

5 red radishes, thinly sliced with a mandolin
2 pickling cucumbers, sliced with a mandolin, (I like Kirbys)
½ Vidalia, Walla Walla or other sweet onion, sliced with a mandolin
¼ cup fresh cilantro, minced
1 teaspoon pink peppercorns
¼ cup apple cider vinegar
¾ tablespoon sugar
1 teaspoon ginger juice
¼ teaspoon sea salt

Combine radishes, cucumbers, onion, cilantro and peppercorns in a medium mixing bowl and set aside.

In a small saucepan over medium heat, combine vinegar, sugar, ginger juice and salt. Bring to a boil and stir constantly to dissolve sugar. Pour over vegetables and toss well. Refrigerate 20 minutes, stirring a couple of times. Transfer to a Mason jar and seal. Store in the refrigerator and use within one month.

Cilantro Pesto #1

Serve on baked or roasted potatoes, grilled vegetables, as a sandwich spread, and of course, on pasta.
Makes 2 cups.

½ cup pumpkin seeds
2½ cups gently packed fresh cilantro, leaves and stems
2 cups walnuts
½ cup packed fresh parsley
2 cloves garlic
¼ cup plus 1 tablespoon fresh lemon juice
2 teaspoons paprika
1 teaspoon sea salt
1 teaspoon red pepper flakes
½ cup plus 2 tablespoons extra virgin olive oil
2 tablespoons nutritional yeast

Bring a small, dry frying pan to medium heat. Add pumpkin seeds and stir continuously as they start to pop. When browned, transfer to a plate to cool.

In a food processor, combine cilantro, walnuts, parsley, garlic, lemon juice, paprika, salt and red pepper flakes and purée. Add pumpkin seeds and process until smooth, scraping down sides as needed. With machine running, pour oil in a steady stream and process until incorporated. Add water to thin to desired consistency. Taste and adjust seasoning.

Cilantro Pesto #2

Lightly adapted from Jean-Marie Josselin's A Tate of Hawaii. Definitely more zing than Pesto #1, but there's a place for both. In addition to pasta, use as a dip, sweet potato topping or bagel schmear.
Makes 1 cup.

1 cup chopped fresh cilantro
½ cup minced fresh ginger
½ cup sliced scallions
1 teaspoon minced garlic
1/3 cup peanut oil
2 teaspoons sesame oil
½ teaspoon sea salt
¼ teaspoon freshly ground black pepper
2 tablespoons fresh lemon juice
1 tablespoon *Vegan Parmesan* (in Basics)

In a small bowl, combine cilantro, ginger, scallions and garlic. Mix well and set aside.

In a saucepan, heat peanut and sesame oils until hot. Pour over cilantro mixture. Add salt, pepper and lemon juice and process with a stick blender. Stir in vegan parmesan and mix well. Taste and adjust seasoning. Refrigerate until ready to use.

Chilled Coconut and Lettuce Soup with Cilantro

I love an unusual combination of ingredients, especially when they taste so natural together. This is a refreshing chilled soup, the antidote for those dog days of summer.

Makes ~8 cups, 6-8 servings.

½ head iceberg lettuce cored
1 cup shredded unsweetened coconut
3 cups non-dairy milk
¾ cup gently packed cilantro plus more to garnish
¼ cup all-purpose flour
2 tablespoons minced fresh ginger
3 cups vegetable stock
2 tablespoons minced yellow bell pepper, to garnish
Freshly ground black pepper, to garnish

Shred enough lettuce to measure 2 cups. Place in a medium bowl, cover and chill.

Bring a large stockpot to medium heat. Combine coconut, non-dairy milk, cilantro, flour and ginger and whisk to dissolve any lumps. Add stock and bring to a boil, stirring often. Remove from heat, cover and let stand 1 hour.

Strain out solids, pressing to extract as much flavor as possible, and discard. Transfer to a high-speed blender with reserved chilled lettuce and purée. Taste and adjust seasoning. Chill thoroughly before serving and garnish with minced bell pepper, freshly ground black pepper and additional cilantro.

Marinated Black Beans with Jalapeño and Cilantro

This salad has everything--protein, complex carbs, good fat, color, texture, and lots of flavor. It travels well too. #VeganCincoDeMayo
Makes 6-8 servings.

Two 15-ounce cans black beans, rinsed and drained well
3 green onions, both white and green parts, sliced thinly on the diagonal
1 red, yellow or orange bell pepper, diced
½ cup fresh cut corn from the cob
1 jalapeño, seeded and minced
¾ cup fresh cilantro, minced
¼ cup fresh lemon or lime juice
¼ cup extra-virgin olive oil or *No-Oil Oil* (in Basics)
2 teaspoons minced garlic
½ teaspoon sea salt
¼ teaspoon freshly ground black pepper
1/8 teaspoon cayenne
1 tablespoon cumin seeds

Place beans in a large serving bowl and add onions, bell peppers, corn, jalapeño, cilantro and stir well to mix.

In a small bowl, mix together citrus juice, oil, garlic, salt, black pepper and cayenne. Pour over beans and use a rubber spatula to mix well and coat vegetables. Taste and adjust seasoning.

Bring a small, dry frying pan to medium-high heat. Add cumin seeds and toast 60-90 seconds, stirring constantly. Add to bean mixture and stir to incorporate. Refrigerate at least 20 minutes before serving.

Raw Beet and Rhubarb Slaw with Cilantro Dressing

When mixed with the rest of these ingredients, rhubarb isn't tart, and when grated, it's just plain easier to eat. #IHeartRhubarb
Makes 4-6 servings.

¼ cup raw pumpkin seeds
1 cup size amount raw rhubarb, ends trimmed
1 cup size amount raw red beets, peeled
1 cup size amount raw red cabbage
1 cup size amount raw carrots, scrubbed clean or peeled
¼ cup thinly sliced green onions, cut on the diagonal
1 cup fresh cilantro, leaves and stems
2½ tablespoons extra-virgin olive oil or *No-Oil Oil* (in Basics)
2½ tablespoons rice vinegar
2 tablespoons fresh orange juice
1 tablespoon agave
1 tablespoon-size rough chopped peeled ginger
½ teaspoon sea salt

Bring a medium, dry frying pan to medium-high heat. Add pumpkin seeds and toast a couple of minutes until lightly browned, stirring regularly. Remove from pan and set aside to cool.

Use the shredder disc in a food processor and grate rhubarb, beets, cabbage and carrots in batches. Transfer to a large mixing bowl and add green onions. Toss to mix well and set aside.

In a mini-blender, process cilantro, oil, vinegar, orange juice, agave, ginger and salt until smooth. Taste and adjust seasoning. Pour over vegetables and toss to incorporate. Refrigerate one hour before serving.

Baked Apple Rings with Curry and Cilantro

My new favorite healthy snack! Use a mandolin to cut the apple thinly, otherwise they'll take even longer to bake. (Four hours is long enough.) If you don't want to make your own sauce, use a favorite jarred curry. #4HourTransformation

Makes 4–6 servings.

3 tablespoons full fat canned coconut milk

1 tablespoon water

1 tablespoon cilantro, ground in a spice grinder

1 tablespoon fresh lime juice

2 teaspoons vanilla paste (not extract)

1 teaspoon curry powder

1 teaspoon unsweetened shredded coconut, finely ground in a spice grinder

¼ teaspoon ginger powder

½ teaspoon onion powder

¼ teaspoon garlic powder

¼ teaspoon turmeric

4 of your favorite sweet or crisp apples, skins scrubbed clean and cored

Preheat oven to 200°F. Line four large cookie sheets with parchment and set aside.

In a small bowl, mix coconut milk, water, cilantro, lime juice, vanilla paste, curry, coconut, ginger, onion, garlic, and turmeric. Taste and adjust seasoning. Mix well and set aside. This makes enough for a few batches.

Freeze leftover sauce and you'll be ready to make more in the fall, when other varieties of apples are in season.

Slice apples with a mandolin, discarding (or eating) the top and bottom slice of each apple. Those slices have too much skin to lay flat and not enough surface area to coat with the coconut mixture. Lay apple rings in a single layer on prepared sheets. Crowd them together but do not overlap. One apple will fill an entire cookie sheet.

Use your fingers or the back of a small spoon to lightly coat the tops with the coconut mixture. They just need to get wet, not thickly coated. Bake for one hour. Remove from oven, turn over and coat the other side. You're done with the sauce, so refrigerate for a later batch. Return to oven and bake 1 hour. You're at hour two.

Remove from oven and turn again. It doesn't look like much is happening, but the magic happens in the final hour. Bake one hour, (hour 3), turn rings and repeat one final hour. Apple rings should be dry and crispy. Go on, take a bite and test one. If it's chewy at all, keep cooking. Cool a couple of minutes before consuming. Store in a tightly sealed container in the refrigerator.

Pea and Asparagus Guacamole with Cilantro
This guacamole is a great source of protein, thanks to the peas. Just as important, it retains its lively green color, meaning leftovers won't turn that disturbing, unappetizing brown color. #99ProblemsButProteinAin'tOne Makes 4 cups.

20 fresh, thin, green asparagus spears, cleaned and trimmed
1 pound frozen peas, thawed
1 cup fresh cilantro
2 garlic cloves
½ teaspoon red pepper flakes
¼ cup lemon juice
3 tablespoons extra-virgin olive oil or *No-Oil Oil* (in Basics)
1 teaspoon cumin
½ teaspoon sea salt
¼ teaspoon freshly ground black pepper
1 cup seeded and diced tomato
½ cup diced red onion
2-4 tablespoons minced jalapeño
1/3 cup sliced black olives, to garnish

In a small saucepan, bring ½ cup water to a boil. Add asparagus, reduce heat, cover and simmer ~5 minutes, or until tender. Use a spider strainer to remove asparagus to an ice bath. Drain and set aside.

In a food processor, purée peas, cilantro, garlic, red pepper flakes, lemon juice, oil, cumin, salt and black pepper. Add drained asparagus, and process until smooth. Transfer to a medium bowl.

Stir in tomato, red onion and jalapeño. Taste and adjust seasoning. Cover and refrigerate an hour before serving. Garnish with black olives.

Indian-Spiced Cashews with Cilantro

Cashews provide the perfect creamy background for these seasonings. A little sweet, a little tang--these nuts are good solo or added to salads or grain bowls. #Warning:Addictive
Makes 1½ cups.

½ cup gently packed fresh cilantro, leaves and stems, rinsed and patted
  dry
¼ cup golden raisins
½ tablespoon fresh garlic
1½ cups raw cashews halves or large pieces (not whole)
1 tablespoon organic, cold-pressed, unrefined coconut oil
1½ tablespoons lime juice
½ teaspoon sugar
½ teaspoon garam masala
¼ teaspoon sea salt

Move one rack to the middle of the oven and preheat to 350°F.

In a food processor, process cilantro, raisins and garlic until finely minced.

Bring a large, dry sauté pan to medium heat. Add nuts and stir regularly for 3 minutes, or until lightly toasted. Transfer to a plate or rimmed baking sheet to cool.

In the same sauté pan but with the heat off, add oil, lime juice, sugar, garam masala and salt. Stir well to combine. Add cilantro mixture and stir to combine. Add nuts, being careful not to add any little burnt flakes. Mix well to coat completely.

Spread nuts in a single layer on rimmed cookie sheet and place on the middle rack. There might be some globby areas, but spreading the nuts out helps that to dry. Bake 5 minutes, remove and stir. Return to oven for 3 minutes, this time on the lowest rack. Remove and stir again. Repeat this process once more. Remove from oven and transfer to a plate to cool. Store in a sealed container in the refrigerator.

Corn Pie with Tomatillo-Cilantro Salsa

This makes a nice brunch or dinner. Use any leftover salsa on cornbread, muffins or baked sweet potatoes.
Pie makes 4-6 servings; salsa makes a generous 2 cups.

3 ears fresh corn
½ cup silken tofu, drained
¼ cup sugar
¼ cup gently packed cilantro
2 tablespoons packed parsley
1 tablespoon non-dairy butter, melted
2 teaspoons freshly minced garlic
1½ teaspoons salt
½ teaspoon baking powder
1 teaspoon cumin
1 teaspoon apple cider vinegar
½ teaspoon black pepper
¼ teaspoon cayenne
½ cup cornmeal
¼ cup minced yellow bell pepper
¼ cup minced red onion
Tomatillo Cilantro Salsa, recipe follows

Preheat oven to 375°F. Lightly grease a 9-inch pie plate with non-stick spray and set aside.

Cut kernels from corn cobs with a sharp knife. Reserve ¼ cup and transfer rest to a food processor. Add tofu, sugar, cilantro, parsley, non-dairy butter, garlic, salt, baking powder, cumin, apple cider vinegar, pepper and cayenne and process until smooth.

Add cornmeal and process to incorporate.

Transfer to a large mixing bowl and fold in bell pepper, onion and reserved corn. Pour into prepared baking dish, pressing to smooth the top and pack it down. Bake 45–50 minutes, or when pie is browned around the edges and a toothpick inserted into the center comes out clean. Cool 10 minutes before cutting into 6–8 wedges. Serve with Tomatillo Cilantro Salsa.

Tomatillo Cilantro Salsa
3 medium tomatillos, husks and stems removed, scrubbed clean and rough chopped
2 large ripe yellow tomatoes, peeled, seeded and rough chopped
1 medium jalapeño, seeded and rough chopped
½ cup gently packed cilantro
½ teaspoon minced garlic
½ teaspoon lemon juice
½ teaspoon sea salt
¼ teaspoon black pepper
¼ cup red onion, minced
1 teaspoon extra-virgin olive oil or *No-Oil Oil* (in Basics)

Place tomatillos, tomatoes, jalapeño, cilantro, garlic, lemon juice, salt and pepper in a food processor and pulse until most of the juices have been released, keeping a little texture. Transfer to a serving bowl and stir in red onion and oil. Taste and adjust seasoning.

Chile and Cilantro-Infused Vinegar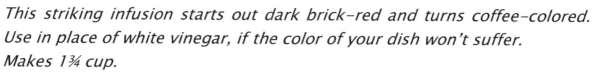

This striking infusion starts out dark brick-red and turns coffee-colored. Use in place of white vinegar, if the color of your dish won't suffer. Makes 1¾ cup.

1¾ cups white wine vinegar
½ cup fresh cilantro, leaves and stems
2 dried Anaheim or California chiles, ~4" in length
2 whole garlic cloves, slightly mashed but whole
Zest and juice of ½ a lime
1 pint Mason jar

In a medium saucepan, add vinegar and bring just to a boil. Remove from heat. Place cilantro, chiles, garlic, zest and juice in a Mason jar and pour warmed vinegar on top. Make sure everything is completely submerged. Cool completely before sealing. Place in a warm, dark place for one week, shaking gently daily.

Strain off solids and discard. Strain vinegar into a clean jar. Store in refrigerator and use within 2 months.

Cilantro and Chile-Infused Vinaigrette
½ cup cilantro-infused chili vinegar (above)
¼ cup extra-virgin olive oil or *No-Oil Oil* (in Basics)
2 tablespoons sugar
2 tablespoons fresh lime juice
2 teaspoons prepared yellow mustard
¼ teaspoon sea salt
¼ cup fresh cilantro leaves, roughly chopped

In a small saucepan, combine vinegar, oil, sugar, lime juice, mustard and salt. Bring to a boil, stirring to dissolve sugar and mix well. Remove from heat and cool completely. Stir in cilantro before serving. Store in refrigerator in a sealed container.

Roasted Sweet Potatoes with Cilantro-Garlic Sauce

Known as the pepper used to make chile rellenos, poblanos are distinctly dark green in color and consistently mild in flavor. That's what makes them work so well with other vegetables. If you need a substitute, use Anaheim or pasilla chile.

Makes 4 servings.

3 pounds sweet potatoes, skins scrubbed clean and cut into 1" chunks
2 tablespoons organic, cold-pressed, unrefined coconut oil, melted
1¼ teaspoons sea salt, divided
¾ teaspoon freshly ground black pepper, divided
¼ cup pumpkin seeds
½ red onion, quartered and sliced
½ pound poblano chiles, stemmed, seeded and cut into ¼" strips
1 cup fresh cilantro, leaves and stems
1 tablespoon fresh garlic
3 tablespoons fresh lime juice
2 tablespoons plain non-dairy yogurt
1 tablespoon apple cider vinegar

Preheat oven to 400°F. Line a rimmed baking pan with parchment and set aside.

Place sweet potato chunks in a large mixing bowl and add oil. Toss well to thoroughly coat. Add 1 teaspoon salt and ½ teaspoon black pepper and stir. Place on prepared baking pan and bake 20 minutes.

Meanwhile, bring a medium, dry skillet to medium heat. Add pumpkin seeds and toast, stirring regularly for 4–5 minutes. Remove from heat, transfer to a small plate to cool and set aside.

Remove sweet potatoes from oven and add red onion and poblano slices to the pan. Stir to mix well, return to oven and cook15 minutes. Remove from oven, stir and return to oven for 5 more minutes, or until onion and poblanos are soft and potatoes are fork-tender. Transfer to a large serving dish and keep warm.

In a small bowl with a stick blender, combine cilantro, garlic, lime juice, non-dairy yogurt, apple cider vinegar, remaining ¼ teaspoon salt and ¼ teaspoon pepper. Process until well mixed. Taste and adjust seasoning. Transfer to a small bowl and spoon a goodly amount over potato mixture. Serve remainder alongside. Sprinkle with toasted pepitas and serve.

Eggplant with Miso Sauce and Cilantro

Lightly adapted from VegetarianTimes.com If you have leftovers, throw them in a high-speed blender with a bit of coconut milk, some chopped onion, a pinch turmeric and black mustard seeds and whip yourself up a quick soup. #Recycle

Makes 4 servings.

2 tablespoons white miso
2 tablespoons dry white wine
1 tablespoon sugar
1 tablespoon rice wine vinegar
1 teaspoon freshly grated ginger
4 small American eggplant
1 tablespoon sesame oil
Sea salt
1 tablespoon tahini
1 tablespoon black sesame seeds
1 green onion, green part only, thinly sliced on the diagonal
½ cup fresh cilantro, minced

In a small saucepan, whisk together miso, wine, sugar, vinegar and ginger and bring to medium heat. Cook 2 minutes to thicken. Remove from heat and set aside.

Pre-heat oven to 400°F and position a rack in the middle.

Remove stems from eggplant and cut in half lengthwise. Score the flesh in a crisscross pattern and brush with sesame oil.

Sprinkle with a little sea salt and place cut side up on a rimmed baking sheet. Roast 20 minutes, then turn over and roast 10 more minutes.

Move rack to highest position in the oven and change temperature to broil. Turn eggplant over and brush cut sides with miso mixture. Return to oven and broil 4–5 minutes.

Transfer to serving dish and drizzle with tahini, sprinkle with sesame seeds, green onions and cilantro.

Green Chile Brownies with Cilantro

Bananas stand in for eggs as the binding ingredient in this recipe. If you use frozen, the additional moisture won't create the typical brownie "cracks" across the surface. If it's heat you want, substitute half the green chiles with freshly minced jalapeño. Use at your own risk!
#NotAllJalapeñosTasteAlike
Makes 12 squares.

2 tablespoons flax meal
2/3 cup non-dairy semisweet chocolate chips
¼ cup organic, cold-pressed, unrefined coconut oil
2½ tablespoons non-dairy butter
2 ripe or frozen bananas
1 cup maple sugar
¾ teaspoon vanilla extract
1¼ cups sprouted spelt flour or all-purpose
¼ cup unsweetened cocoa powder
½ teaspoon sea salt
¼ teaspoon chili powder
6 ounces canned mild diced green chiles, well drained
¾ cup fresh cilantro, minced

In a large mixing bowl, mix flax meal with 5 tablespoons water and set aside.

Preheat oven to 350°F. Spray a 9-by-13-inch baking pan lightly with non-stick spray and set aside.

Use a double boiler to melt the non-dairy chocolate chips, coconut oil and non-dairy butter together, and stir well to combine. Remove from heat and transfer to a large mixing bowl. Set aside to cool.

Add bananas to flax meal and use a stick blender to mash well. Add sugar and vanilla and blend well to incorporate. Add to chocolate mixture and mix well with a rubber spatula.

Add flour, cocoa powder, salt and chili powder and mix until almost blended. Fold in chiles and cilantro.

Transfer batter to prepared baking pan and bake 40 minutes, until a toothpick inserted in the center comes out just a little moist. If you used frozen bananas, this might take a little longer. Cool completely before cutting.

Banana-Lentil Soup with Cilantro

My adaptation of Doug Richardson's rich, nourishing soup. The cute, little Manzano bananas, (also called apple bananas), can be found in international markets. They break down during the cooking process and add just a hint of sweetness. That makes the ingredients trickier for people to identify. #SoupSurprise
Makes 6 servings.

¾ tablespoon organic, cold-pressed, unrefined coconut oil

1 medium yellow onion, finely chopped

1 cup finely chopped celery

¾ tablespoon minced garlic

¼ cup tomato paste

3 cups vegetable stock

2½ cups water

1 cup uncooked brown lentils, rinsed and picked over

½ teaspoon sea salt

¼ teaspoon black pepper

½ cup fresh cilantro, rough chopped, divided

2 ripe Manzano bananas or 1 large just-ripe regular banana

Bring a large stockpot to medium heat. Add oil to coat the bottom. Add onions, celery and garlic and cook 7 minutes, or until soft. Add tomato paste and cook another 2 minutes. Add stock and water and bring to a boil. Lower to a simmer, add lentils, salt and pepper and cover. Cook one hour.

Peel bananas and slice bananas into 1" coins. Quarter slices and add to soup along with half the cilantro and stir. Taste and adjust seasoning. Simmer 10 minutes, stirring occasionally. Serve warm, garnished with remaining cilantro.

Quick Watermelon-Cilantro Soup

Processing cilantro with the watermelon incorporates the flavors better, but it also muddies the color. I've compromised a little bit here--blending some and garnishing with the rest. #WhenYouCan'tInfuse,Blend
Makes 5 cups, 4-6 servings.

7 cups ripe watermelon, roughly chopped
2 teaspoon-size garlic
2 tablespoons fresh lemon juice
2 tablespoons fresh lime juice
¼ cup minced red onion, divided
½ teaspoon sea salt
½ cup gently packed fresh cilantro leaves, minced, divided
8-10 leaves baby arugula, to garnish

In a high-speed blender, process watermelon, garlic, lemon juice, half the red onion, salt and ¼ cup cilantro until well blended. Taste and adjust seasoning. Cover and refrigerate until serving. Serve in chilled bowls, topped with remaining cilantro and a couple of arugula leaves.

Sweet Cilantro Dressing

This works well over sliced stone fruit and berries, for breakfast or dessert.
#NowForSomethingCompletelyDifferent
Makes ~1 cup.

¼ cup shallot, rough chopped
¼ cup orange juice
½ ripe banana, rough chopped
¼ cup extra-virgin olive oil or *No-Oil Oil* (in Basics)
½ cup gently packed fresh cilantro, leaves and stems
1 tablespoon lime juice
1½ teaspoons size fresh garlic
¼ teaspoon sea salt
Freshly ground black pepper to taste

In a high-speed blender, process shallot, orange juice, banana, oil, cilantro, lime juice, garlic, salt and black pepper until smooth. Taste and adjust seasoning. Refrigerate to chill until serving, at least 20 minutes.

Quinoa and Cilantro Neat Loaf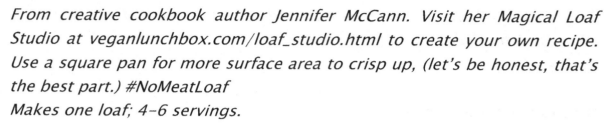

From creative cookbook author Jennifer McCann. Visit her Magical Loaf Studio at veganlunchbox.com/loaf_studio.html to create your own recipe. Use a square pan for more surface area to crisp up, (let's be honest, that's the best part.) #NoMeatLoaf
Makes one loaf; 4-6 servings.

½ cup raw pumpkin seeds
¾ tablespoon organic, cold-pressed, unrefined coconut oil
1 cup small dice yellow onion
1 cup diced celery
¾ cup grated carrot
1½ teaspoons minced garlic
One 15.5-ounce can black eye peas or any beans, reserving liquid
1 cup cooked quinoa
¼–½ cup liquid from the black eye pea or bean can
½ cup yellow cornmeal
1/3 cup black olives, rough chopped
½ cup fresh cilantro, minced
¼ cup fresh parsley, minced
2 tablespoons soy sauce
1 tablespoon vegan Worcestershire sauce
Freshly ground black pepper, to taste

Preheat oven to 350°F. Spray a loaf pan or an 8-inch square pan with non-stick cooking spray and set aside.

In a food processor, process pumpkin seeds into a coarse meal. Set aside.

Bring a large frying pan to medium-high heat. Add oil, onion, celery, carrot and garlic. Stir to incorporate and lower heat to medium. Cover and cook 10-12 minutes, stirring once, until soft.

Rinse beans and drain, reserving can liquid. Add beans to a large mixing bowl, and mix with quinoa, ¼ cup canned bean liquid, cornmeal, olives, cilantro, parsley, soy sauce, Worcestershire, black pepper and ground pumpkin seeds. Mix together well, adding more canned bean liquid to create a soft, moist loaf that hold together and is not runny. Add more quinoa or cornmeal if loaf seems too wet. Taste and adjust seasoning.

Press mixture into prepared pan and bake 45 minutes to 1 hour, or until cooked through. Sorry for the broad range, but there's too much moisture variability in the components to pinpoint it more accurately. You'll learn by doing, and you may like it more moist or drier than I. The sides and top should be nice and browned and the sides have pulled away from the pan slightly.

Cool loaf in pan 10-15 minutes, then turn out onto a plate and slice. Serve with potatoes, vegetables and salsa, if desired.

Verde Claro Soup with Cilantro

I've taken traditional white soup and put a cilantro spin on it, which makes it naturally green. It's a sophisticated little soup, and quite beautiful to the eye. It's also good as a cold soup. #ColorMeGreen
Makes 6-8 servings.

6 cups non-dairy milk, divided
1½ cups cilantro, leaves and stems, gently packed, divided
¼ cup minced shallot
¼ cup minced celery
3-5 whole, small inside stalks of celery, leaves and all
1 tablespoon minced garlic
1 tablespoon minced jalapeño, divided
½ teaspoon sea salt
¼ teaspoon white pepper
1 tablespoon fresh lemon zest
1 radish, thinly sliced with a mandolin, to garnish
¼ ear fresh corn kernels, to garnish

In a high-speed blender, combine 3 cups non-dairy milk with 1 cup cilantro, and process until there are no visible cilantro flecks. Pour into a medium stockpot and add remaining non-dairy milk, ½ cup cilantro, shallot, both minced and whole celery, garlic, half the jalapeño, salt and white pepper.

Bring to a low boil over medium heat, then lower to a simmer and cook 15 minutes, stirring occasionally. Taste and adjust seasoning. Remove from heat and stir in lemon zest.

Now you have options: serve the soup as is or strain off the solids and discard. I like it both ways but straining everything out makes it more sophisticated. Top each bowl with a couple radish slices and a pinch corn kernels.

Watermelon Salad with Bean Sprouts and Cilantro

Reserve the watermelon shell to use as the serving bowl. The recipe makes a little more salad than the shell can hold, but it's actually more appealing having it spill out onto the plate. #WatermelonBowl=QuickCleanUp
Makes 6–8 servings.

1 small watermelon, cut with a melon baller (½" is a nice size)
1 cup roughly chopped cilantro
1 cup fresh bean sprouts
1 clove garlic, minced
½ teaspoon smoked, hot paprika (not sweet)
½ cups unsalted roasted peanuts, rough chopped

After making the melon balls, hollow out the watermelon and refrigerate until ready to serve.

In a large mixing bowl, add watermelon balls, cilantro, bean sprouts, garlic and paprika. Season with a little salt and toss gently to mix. Transfer to the chilled watermelon. Sprinkle with peanuts and serve.

Pickled Rhubarb with Cilantro

I add these to tossed salads for their color, texture and zing. Be prepared for people to ask what they're eating. #LooksLikePinkCelery
Makes 2 cups.

2 cups rhubarb, cut into ¼" slices on the diagonal
½ cup cilantro, leaves and stems, rinsed well and patted dry
1 cup champagne vinegar
½ cup sugar
¾ teaspoon sea salt

Place chopped rhubarb and cilantro in a large Mason jar and set aside.

In a small saucepan, combine vinegar, sugar, salt and ¾ cup water and bring to a boil. Stir to dissolve sugar. Pour over rhubarb and seal container. Refrigerate 2 hours, shaking container every half hour or so. Tastes and continue infusing if you'd like a stronger cilantro flavor, up to 2 more hours. Strain off cilantro and discard. Transfer to a clean Mason jar, seal and store refrigerated. Rhubarb will keep for 3 weeks.

Curried Carrot Soup with Cilantro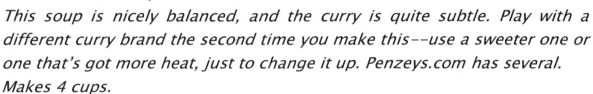

This soup is nicely balanced, and the curry is quite subtle. Play with a different curry brand the second time you make this--use a sweeter one or one that's got more heat, just to change it up. Penzeys.com has several. Makes 4 cups.

2 cups chopped carrots, cut into ¼" coins
1 teaspoon cumin seeds
1½ cups low-salt vegetable broth
½ cup canned coconut milk
¾ cup fresh cilantro, including stems, plus ¼ cup leaves to garnish
1½ teaspoons-size garlic
½ teaspoon curry powder
1 ripe avocado
½ tablespoon fresh ginger, rough chopped
½ teaspoon hot sauce
¾ teaspoon sea salt
¾ teaspoon black pepper
¼ teaspoon turmeric
1 teaspoon fresh lemon juice

Place carrots in a steamer basket over boiling water. Cover and steam 15 minutes. Remove from steamer and place on a large plate to cool.

Bring a small, dry skillet to medium-high heat. Add cumin seeds and toast 60-90 seconds, stirring regularly, until lightly toasted. Remove from pan and set aside.

In a high-speed blender, add broth, coconut milk, ¾ cup cilantro, garlic, curry, avocado, ginger, hot sauce, salt, pepper and turmeric and process until smooth. Add carrots and process again until smooth. Add lemon juice and process 30 seconds. Taste and adjust seasonings. Serve warm, topped with toasted cumin seeds and reserved cilantro.

Cauliflower Patties with Cilantro

If you'd prefer these crispy, fry them on the stove in a little bit of coconut oil.

Makes ~8 patties.

3 cups cauliflower, florets and stems, roughly chopped
3/4 cup plus 2 tablespoons fresh cilantro, including stems
¼ cup green onion, both white and green parts, coarsely chopped
1 tablespoon plus 1½ teaspoon fresh garlic
1½ tablespoons flax meal
1 tablespoon fresh lemon juice
1½ teaspoons freshly grated lemon zest
½ teaspoon sea salt
¼ teaspoon red pepper flakes
¼ teaspoon black pepper
1 cup old fashioned oats
1/3 cup plus 1 tablespoon golden raisins
¼ cup dry roasted peanuts, rough chopped
Cilantro Pesto #1 or 2

Preheat oven to 350°F. Spray a rimmed baking sheet with non-stick spray and set aside.

Place cauliflower in a food processor and process until finely ground. Transfer to a large mixing bowl. In the same food processor, add cilantro, green onion, garlic, flax meal, lemon juice, zest, salt, red pepper flakes and black pepper and process until well blended. Add to cauliflower and stir to incorporate. Stir in oats, raisins and peanuts and mix well. Taste and adjust seasoning.

Shape into equal-sized balls and flatten into hamburger-size patties. Place on prepared baking sheet and flatten evenly with a spatula. Bake 12 minutes. Remove from oven and turn over. Return to oven and cook another 10-12 minutes, until lightly golden. Serve warm with Cilantro Pesto.

Molasses Chili with Cilantro

It's a texture thing. Soy curls provide the texture we expect from a hearty chili. If you don't want soy, substitute seitan. Fry it up with the onion, garlic and jalapeño to give it more depth of flavor. #Seitan=SayTan #Seitan=WheatMeat

Makes 5½ cups; 4 servings.

4 ounces soy curls (Butler Soy Curls are Non-GMO and gluten-free)
½ tablespoon organic, cold-pressed, unrefined coconut oil
1 cup minced onion
1 tablespoon minced garlic
½ jalapeño, minced
One 4.5 ounce can diced green chiles
One 15-ounce can navy beans, rinsed and well-drained
2½ cups water
4 ounces tomato sauce
2 medium tomatoes, diced
½ cup fresh cilantro, minced, divided plus extra to garnish
3 tablespoons molasses
2 tablespoons dark brown sugar
2 tablespoons tomato paste
½ teaspoon cumin
½ teaspoon dry mustard
½ teaspoon sea salt
½ teaspoon black pepper
¼ cup nutritional yeast
2 cups crushed tortilla chips, to garnish

Place soy curls in a medium mixing bowl and cover with warm water. Soak 10 minutes to rehydrate. Drain excess water and set aside.

Bring a large stockpot to medium-high heat. Add oil, onions, garlic and jalapeño and sauté 3 minutes. Add green chiles, beans, water, tomato sauce, diced tomatoes and ½ cup cilantro and bring to a boil. Add in soy curls, stir, lower heat to medium-low and cook 10 minutes.

In a small bowl, mix molasses, brown sugar, tomato paste, cumin, mustard, salt and pepper. Add to stockpot along with nutritional yeast and pepper. Add to stockpot along with nutritional yeast and stir well. Lower heat to a simmer and cook 10 minutes. Serve warm topped with tortilla chips and reserved cilantro.

No-Churn Cilantro Nice Cream

Adapted from Natalie's recipe at FeasingonFruit.com How great is this? No need to haul out an ice cream maker when you can make no-churn nice cream.
#IceCreamDreams
Makes 2¼ cups.

1 cup non-dairy milk, refrigerated
½ large avocado
½ cup unsalted pistachios plus 2 tablespoons cup rough chopped, to garnish
1/3 cup maple syrup
¾ cup fresh cilantro leaves and stems
¼ teaspoon almond extract
Two mini-loaf pans, 3-by-5-inches and 2-inches deep

Line two small loaf pans with parchment or soy-derived wax paper, draping it out the ends and over the sides. Set aside.

In a high-speed blender, combine non-dairy milk, avocado, ½ cup pistachios, maple syrup, cilantro and almond extract until smooth. Taste and adjust seasoning.

Pour mixture into prepared pans, sprinkle with reserved chopped pistachios, and freeze overnight.

Remove from freezer and soften on the countertop 10-15 minutes, or until soft enough to scoop. If you prefer it super creamy, freeze in ice cube trays and process in a high-speed blender until smooth, just before serving.

If you have a good quality chocolate bar handy – and you should, let's just be clear about that – break it into small pieces and add to a small saucepan with 2 tablespoons coconut oil. Bring to low heat and stir to melt together. Pour over softened cilantro nice cream and serve.

Smoky Black-Eyed Pea Dip with Cilantro

Spread on toast points with a shot of Sriracha. #SomeLikeItHot
Makes 2 cups.

1½ teaspoons organic, cold-pressed, unrefined coconut oil
1/3 cup spring onions, green and white parts, rough chopped
2 teaspoons cumin plus more to garnish
One 15-ounce can black-eyed peas, rinsed and well-drained
1 teaspoon minced garlic
½ cup packed fresh cilantro, plus extra leaves to garnish
3 tablespoons lime juice
1 tablespoon-size piece of jalapeño
¾ tablespoon chile powder
½ tablespoon tomato paste
½ teaspoon chipotle powder
½ teaspoon sea salt
¼ cup plain, non-dairy yogurt

Bring a medium sauce pan to medium heat. Add oil, onions and cumin. Stir frequently and cook until onions are soft, 1–1½ minutes. Add drained beans, 1/3 cup water and garlic. Simmer 2 minutes, stirring, until water evaporates. Remove from heat to cool.

In a food processor, process ½ cup cilantro. Add lime juice, jalapeño, chile powder, tomato paste, chipotle powder, salt, non-dairy yogurt and ¼ cup water and process until smooth. Add bean mixture and process until smooth. Add more water to make the desired consistency. Taste and adjust seasoning. Garnish with remaining cilantro and a sprinkle cumin.

Cilantro, Jalapeño and Lime Butter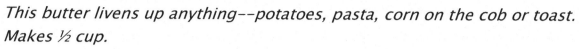

This butter livens up anything--potatoes, pasta, corn on the cob or toast.
Makes ½ cup.

½ cup non-dairy butter, at room temperature
¼ cup packed fresh cilantro, minced
¼ cup fresh chives, minced
1 tablespoon fresh lime juice
1 teaspoon minced jalapeño
1/8 teaspoon garlic powder
Pinch black pepper

In a small mixing bowl, mix non-dairy butter, cilantro, chives, lime juice, jalapeño, garlic and black pepper. Transfer to a small bowl or mold, cover and refrigerate at least an hour. Use within 2 weeks.

Cooked Carrot Salad with Cilantro

Be sure to buy regular sized carrots, otherwise you're sacrificing major flavor for the convenience. The baby carrots that come in plastic bags are pretty tasteless, and boiling them removes whatever flavor they started with. Not so with regular size or organic carrots. This recipe features how awesome carrots can be, with minimal effort and light seasonings.
Makes 4 servings.

6 medium carrots, scrubbed clean, sliced in ¼" coins on the diagonal
1 cup fresh cilantro, minced
½ cup fresh parsley, minced
2 tablespoons fresh lemon juice
1 tablespoon extra-virgin olive oil or *No-Oil Oil* (in Basics)
1 tablespoon plus 1 teaspoon minced fresh garlic
¾ teaspoon sea salt
¾ teaspoon black pepper
½ teaspoon ground cumin
¼ teaspoon cinnamon
¼ teaspoon cayenne

Fill a medium saucepan two-thirds full with water and add a pinch salt. Bring to a boil, add carrots and cook ~7 minutes, until fork-tender. Drain well and transfer to a large bowl. Add cilantro, parsley, lemon juice, oil, garlic, salt, pepper, cumin, cinnamon and cayenne. Toss to mix well and serve immediately.

BASICS

Baconut

Simply the best bacon substitute for garnishing salads, vegetables or soups and in BLTs.

Makes 2 cups.

2 tablespoons reduced sodium soy sauce

1 tablespoon pure Grade B maple syrup

½ teaspoon liquid smoke (I like hickory)

1 tablespoon apple cider vinegar

1 tablespoon organic, cold-pressed, unrefined coconut oil, melted

1 teaspoon smoked paprika

1/8 teaspoon sea salt

2 cups large flake, unsweetened coconut

Preheat oven to 350°F. Place a rack in the middle of the oven. Line a rimmed baking sheet with a silicone mat and set aside.

In a medium mixing bowl, combine soy sauce, maple syrup, liquid smoke, vinegar, oil, paprika and salt and mix well. Stir in coconut flakes and mix well to completely coat.

Spread in a single layer on prepared baking sheet and bake on middle rack for 7 minutes. Remove from oven and stir to turn. Return to oven and cook ~5 minutes, watching closely so they don't burn. Coconut will crisp up after they've cooled completely. Cool completely before storing in an air-tight container in the refrigerator. Use within 1 week.

Brown Gravy

A quick little gravy to go with any form of pasta, potato, vegetable or nut loaf.

Makes ~1½ cups.

2 tablespoons arrowroot
3 tablespoons low-sodium soy sauce
1 and 1/3 cups vegetable broth
1 teaspoon Herbes de Provence
2 tablespoons tahini
1 tablespoon nutritional yeast

In a medium saucepan, combine arrowroot and soy sauce. Gradually whisk in broth and Herbes de Provence. Bring to medium-high heat and cook, stirring constantly with a whisk. Bring to a boil and whisk until thickened.

Remove from heat and whisk in tahini and nutritional yeast. Taste and adjust seasoning. Serve warm.

Coconut Cream

Lightly adapted from the talented Dana Shultz of MinimalistBaker.com. Dollop this sweetened cream on waffles or any dessert, from pie, to pudding and fresh cut fruit.
Makes 1½ cups; 6-8 servings.

One 14-ounce can full fat coconut cream, refrigerated overnight
½-¾ cup powdered sugar
½ teaspoon vanilla paste (not extract)

Place the mixing bowl and whisk attachment in the freezer for half an hour.

Open can and spoon only the hardened cream into chilled bowl. Reserve coconut water for another use. Use a mixer to beat cream for 30 seconds. Scrape down sides and add sugar and vanilla paste. Beat on high until smooth, another minute or so. Use immediately or refrigerate until using. Store in an air-tight container and use within 1 week. Whisk again if necessary before serving.

Creamy White Sauce

This sauce is quite smooth and goes easily over just about anything that needs a sauce--potatoes, grains, greens and nut loafs.
Makes ~4 cups.

2 cups raw cashews, soaked at least 4 hours
1 cup water
1 tablespoon onion powder
1 teaspoon garlic powder
1 teaspoon dried mustard
1 teaspoon smoked paprika
1 teaspoon sea salt
½ teaspoon white pepper
¼ cup fresh lemon juice
2 tablespoons fresh lemon zest
1½ cups non-dairy milk, divided

Drain cashews and add to a high-speed blender with the water. Process until smooth, scraping down the sides as necessary. Add onion and garlic powders, mustard, paprika, salt and pepper and process again. Add lemon juice and zest and process briefly until incorporated. Add one cup non-dairy milk and process again. Keep adding non-dairy milk ¼ cup at a time until you reach the desired consistency. Taste and adjust seasoning.

Gluten–Free Flour Mix

Don't buy a gluten-free flour at the grocery story. This mix has five ingredients! Mix a bowl up and keep it in a sealed container in the refrigerator. If you use it more regularly, keep it in your cupboards.
Makes 3½ cups.

1½ cups brown rice flour
1 cup potato starch
½ cup white rice flour
½ cup tapioca flour (starch)
2 teaspoons xanthan gum

Add the brown rice flour and potato starch to a 1-quart Mason jar. Seal the lid and shake well to combine. Add white rice flour; seal and shake well. Add tapioca and xanthan gum, seal and shake well to combine. Or mix everything up in a large bowl and *then* put it into a Mason jar. Store per your usage as indicated above.

No-Oil Oil

Lightly adapted from Susan Voisin of FatFreeVegan.com. Cut the fat and inflammation. Substitute for any oil used in salad dressings, or when baking, replacing oil up to 1/3 cup. There's no sacrifice to the taste and for things like salad dressings, you still get the weight and texture similar to oil. Double the recipe to have it handy, particularly if you bake a lot. Makes 1½ cups.

1½ cups water
1½ tablespoons cornstarch
¾ teaspoon sea salt

In a high-speed blender, blend water, cornstarch and salt. Pour mixture into a saucepan and whisk as you bring to a boil. Watch carefully to keep it from boiling over. (This can happen fast!) Remove from heat and cool completely. Store in a Mason jar in the refrigerator and use within 2 weeks. Mixture will have the shine and consistency of oil. *#Magic*

Quick Tomato Gravy

We've got a White Sauce and Brown Gravy, so we're rounding out the toppings with something a little extra, a tomato gravy made with chipotles. Add more chipotles or sauce from the can if you like it spicier. Use on potatoes, veggies, tofu scramble, pasta or nut loafs.
Makes ~2½ cups.

½ cup canned chipotle peppers and sauce
½ teaspoon organic, cold-pressed, unrefined coconut oil
½ cup medium-diced onion
1½ teaspoons minced garlic
¼ cup apple cider vinegar
¼ cup brown sugar
2 cups organic ketchup
1 tablespoon nutritional yeast

Place sauce and peppers in a 1 cup measuring cup and use kitchen scissors to cut up any large pieces. Set aside.

Bring a medium saucepan to medium-high heat. Add oil and onion and lower heat to medium-low. Sauté 3 minutes, stirring regularly. Add garlic and stir 30 seconds. Lower heat to lowest setting and add apple cider vinegar and brown sugar. Stir continuously to melt sugar. Add ketchup, nutritional yeast and chipotle peppers and stir well to incorporate. Taste and adjust seasoning. Cook 10 minutes, to reduce slightly and thicken.

Vegan Parmesan

After you've tried the recipe below, play around with it. Customize it with spices you love--paprika, onion powder, cumin, turmeric, black pepper or any dried herb. Use on salads, in salad dressings or soups to thicken, on veggies or pasta sauce. You get the idea. Then make ups a batch or two and keep a Mason jar stocked in the refrigerator. #I'mVersatile
Makes ~2 cups.

1¾ cups raw cashews
¼ cup nutritional yeast
1½ teaspoons sea salt
½ teaspoon garlic powder
1/8 teaspoon paprika

Add nuts to a food processor and pulse until well ground. Add remaining ingredients and pulse to mix well. Taste and adjust seasoning. Store in a Mason jar in the refrigerator.

Resources: For A Deeper Look

Recommended Books

American Wasteland: How America Throws Away Nearly Half of Its Food (and What We Can Do About It), by Jonathan Bloom

Becoming Vegan: The Complete Guide to Adopting a Healthy Plant-Based Diet, by Brenda Davis and Vesanto Melina

The China Study: The Most Comprehensive Study of Nutrition Ever Conducted and the Startling Implications for Diet, Weight Loss, and Long-Term Health, by T. Colin Campbell

Eat Drink Vote: An Illustrated Guide to Food Politics, by Marion Nestle

Eating Animals, by Jonathan Safran Foer

Eat to Live: The Revolutionary Formula for Fast and Sustained Weight Loss, by Dr. Joel Fuhrman

The Ethics of What We Eat, by Peter Singer

Food Fight: The Inside Story of the Food Industry, America's Obesity Crisis, and What We Can Do About It, by Kelly D. Brownell and Katherine Battle Horgen

The Food Revolution: How Your Diet Can Help Save Your Life and Our World, by John Robbins and Dean Ornish, MD

How Not To Die: Discover the Foods Scientifically Proven to Prevent and Reverse Disease, by Michael Greger, MD

Hungry Planet, by Peter Menzel and Faith D'Alusio

In Defense of Food, by Michael Pollan

The Lucky Ones: My Passionate Fight for Farm Animals, by Jenny Brown

Mindless Eating, by Brian Wansink

Pandora's Lunchbox: How Processed Food Took Over the American Meal, by Melanie Warner

Prevent and Reverse Heart Disease: The Revolutionary, Scientifically Proven, Nutrition-Based Cure, by Caldwell B. Esselstyn Jr.

Selling Sickness: How the World's Biggest Pharmaceutical Companies Are Turning Us All Into Patients, by Ray Moynihan and Alan Cassels

Vegan for Life: Everything You Need to Know to be Healthy and Fit on a Plant Based Diet, by Jack Norris, RD and Virginia Messina, MPH, RD

Vegan Freak: Being Vegan in a Non-Vegan World, by Bob Torres and Jenna Torres

What To Eat, by Marion Nestle

Whitewash: The Disturbing Truth About Cow's Milk & Your Health, by Joseph Keon and John Robbins

Why We Love Dogs, Eat Pigs, and Wear Cows, by Melanie Joy, PhD

Recommended Films & Documentaries

Find at your local library, online or through Netflix or other online streaming services.

Cowspiracy: The Sustainability Secret (2014) 1 hour, 31 minutes

Earthlings (2005) 1 hour, 48 minutes

Fat, Sick & Nearly Dead 2 (2014) 1 hour, 28 minutes

Food Inc. (2009) 1 hour, 34 minutes

Forks Over Knives (2011) 1 hour 36 minutes

The Ghost in our Machines (2013) 1 hour 33 minutes

Supersize Me (2004) 1 hour 40 minutes

The Witness (witnessfilm.org) (2000) 43 minutes

Recommended Podcasts

The Bearded Vegans Podcast

Brown Vegan

Eat For The Planet with Nil Zacharias

Food For Thought (Colleen Patrick Goudreau)

Food Heals

No Meat Athlete Radio

Nutrition Facts with Dr. Greger

Our Hen House

The Rich Roll Podcast

Vegan Warrior Princesses Attack

Recommended Websites

Find videos, scientific papers, recipes, live-in programs, restaurant reviews, magazines, events and more.

ChicVegan.com

ColleenPatrickGoudreau.com

DrFuhrman.com

DrMcdougall.com

EatUnprocessed.com

eCornell.com (plant-based nutrition certificate)

DoctorKlaper.com

DrEsselstyn.com

FarmSanctuary.org

FatFreeVegan.com

ForksOverKnives.com

FriendsofAnimals.org

GoVegan.net

HappyCow.net

HumaneSociety.org

IsaChandra.com

JeffNovick.com

JoyfulVegan.com

KrisCarr.com

MeatlessMonday.com

MercyforAnimals.org

MontgomeryHeart.com

NAVS-online.org (North American Vegetarian Society)

NutritionFacts.org

OneGreenPlanet.org

PCRM.org

PlantBasedDoctors.org

VeganBlogger.com

VeganFeastKitchen.blogspot.com

VegNews.com

VegSource.com

Index

55891214R00122

Made in the USA
Columbia, SC
18 April 2019